Acclaim for *I Tell You A Mystery*

Jonathan Kozol, author, *Amazing Grace*

A beautiful book of surpassing dignity and tenderness…I hope it will be widely read, not only by those who call themselves religious. Although written with great simplicity of style, it is nonetheless a work of moral mystery…a small treasure, unpretentious and transcendent.

Paul Brand, M.D. author, *Pain: The Gift Nobody Wants*

I have read many books about dying, but this is the one I would give to someone approaching death or facing bereavement. From start to finish it shines with hope! I want a copy beside my bed when my time comes.

J.I. Packer, Regent College

Modern Christians often fail to face death well. Arnold's book shares golden wisdom on facing it in faith, hope, and love. The true meaning of death with dignity is here writ large.

Benedict Groeschel, C.F.R. Archdiocese of New York

Engaging and challenging. I found myself say "yes" chapter after chapter. A witness to the power of faith.

Dave & Jan Dravecky, co-authors, *When You Can't Come Back*

The stories remind us that in confronting death we are not alone and that we truly have nothing to fear.

Daniel Callahan, Hastings Center

A sensitive, compassionate book…full of faith. Provides insight and wisdom at a time when the care of the dying is a matter of trouble and uncertainty.

John Dear, S.J. author, *The God of Peace*

Challenges me to confront my own fear of death…Arnold's stories encourage me to embrace the God of life. They are a great comfort.

Brennan Manning, author, *The Ragamuffin Gospel*

Arnold's portraits compel us to address the depth of our commitment to the resurrection promise.

Vernon Grounds, Denver Seminary

I have found this book invaluable in my counseling and pastoral ministry. It stirs, yes awakens, the soul, not only of those who nervously avoid the question of death – or of those who care for the terminally ill – but of us all.

Cicely Saunders, Founder, St. Christopher's Hospice, London

There are many books available by people bereaved of someone they loved, but the fact that this one comes from the Bruderhof community gives it a special strength.

Milton W. Hay, National Council of Hospice Professionals

Arnold reveals a heart acquainted with grief. He invites the reader to journey with men, women, boys and girls whose poignant stories of death and loss provide an extraordinarily helpful clinical and inspirational resource. To accept the invitation is to come upon an almost unbearably widened vista of living.

Thomas Howard, author, *Christ the Tiger: A Postscript to Dogma*

Distinguished from other books about death by its candor, simplicity, and courage.

Richard Rohr, O.F.M. Center for Action and Contemplation

Our secular culture sees death as a unwelcome and too early visitor. We have been given a great and liberating path through this dark mystery – not only by Jesus but by these who follow in the "great parade." Read and rejoice!

Mary E. O'Brien, University of North Carolina

I Tell You a Mystery should be required reading for anyone in the healthcare professions and for anyone in search of the answers to life's most baffling questions.

Rev. William Grosch, M.D. Capital District Psychiatric Center

A gem of a book…Speaks volumes about God's love, despite threatening illness…Reading this book made me cry tears of sadness as well as joy. I commend it to all those in the helping professions.

Fr. Mark S. Begly, St. John the Baptist Parish

…Resists the temptation of offering instantaneous and easy answers to the bewildering questions surround the mystery of death. My parishioners will be able to connect with these stories and Arnold's uncomplicated style immediately…I will use it often in my ministry.

I Tell You A Mystery

I Tell You A Mystery

Life, Death, and Eternity

Johann Christoph Arnold

Foreword by Madeleine L'Engle

The Plough Publishing House

©1996 by The Plough Publishing House
of The Bruderhof Foundation

Farmington PA 15437 USA
Robertsbridge, E. Sussex, TN32 5DR UK

Foreword by Madeleine L'Engle ©1996 by Crosswicks, Ltd.
Cover photograph ©1996 by Farrell Grehan
I wish to thank all those who faithfully worked day and night to assist me
in putting this book together: Ellen Keiderling, Hanna Rimes, Emmy Maria Blough,
Emmy Barth, Hela Ehrlich, Jonathan Zimmerman, and Chris Zimmerman for their
editorial and secretarial support; Emily Alexander, Clare Stober for the artwork
and design; and most of all Madeleine L'Engle, for her Foreword.

First printing 10,000   Oct. 1996
Second printing 15,000   Dec. 1996
Third printing 5,000   Apr. 1999

A catalog record for this book is available from the British Library.

Library of Congress Cataloging-in-Publication Data

Arnold, Johann Christoph, 1940 –
    I tell you a mystery : life, death, and eternity / Johann Christoph Arnold;
    Foreword by Madeleine L'Engle.
       p. cm.
    Includes bibliographical references.
    ISBN 0-87486-083-0 (pbk.)
    1. Bruderhof Communities   2. Death--Religious aspects--Bruderhof
Communities.   3. Bruderhof Communities--Death.   I. Title.
BX8129.B64A84   1997
289.7'3--DC21   96-44035
                                                          CIP

Printed in the USA

LO! I tell you a mystery.
We shall not all sleep,
but we shall all be changed.

1 Cor. 15:51

TO MY GRANDCHILDREN, and to all children,
in the hope that these stories of faith and courage
may be an example to you. We live in a time of peace
and plenty, but there is no guarantee that it will always
be so. If we live in full surrender to God – if we live for
love – he will walk with us, lifting us when we fall and
protecting us in every situation. If we open our lives to
him, he will work in us as he did in the lives of the people
whose stories make up this book.

Contents

Foreword

ONE EVENING while my children were doing homework, I was sitting at my desk, writing, when one of our young neighbors, high school age, came in demanding, "Madeleine, are you afraid of death?"

Barely turning I answered, "Yes, Bob, of course." He plunked himself down on a chair. "Oh, thank God. Nobody else has dared admit it."

Death is change, and change is always fearful as well as challenging, but until we can admit the fear, we cannot accept the challenge. Until we can admit the fear, we cannot know the assurance, deep down in our hearts, that indeed, we are *not* afraid.

I Tell You A Mystery is a wonderful book of the kind of fearlessness of death that comes with our normal fear, no matter how deep our faith. Indeed, it is only deep faith that can admit fear, and then move on to the understand-

ing that God can
work through our
tragedies as well as
our joys; that even
when accidents and
illness let us down,
God never lets us
down.

I am also grateful
that *I Tell You A Mystery* addresses the paradox of our abuse
of the great gift of free will, and God's working out of
Love's plan for the universe. No, God does not cause or
will the death of a child, but God can come into all things,
no matter how terrible. God can help us to bear them, and
even be part of them, especially if we live in community,
whether community such as the Bruderhof, or the smaller,
less structured community of our churches.

In a society that is afraid of death – not the normal fear
Bob expressed, but the terrible fear that surrounds us when
we are not centered on God – we tend to isolate the dying,
implying that death is contagious. Yes, we all die; there are
no exceptions; but we are not meant to die alone. I was
taken through a beautiful new cancer hospital where in
each room there was what looked like a small mahogany
table. In a moment it could be pulled out and turned into
a bed, where a family member or friend could be with the
person who was ill.

I was privileged to be with my husband, holding him, at
the time of his death. The grace to be with other people as

they have made the great transition has been given me. Perhaps when I answered Bob's question with, "Yes, of course," I was referring to awe, rather than fear or panic, an awe some of us are afraid to face.

I wish a friend had put this beautiful book in my hands when my husband died. It honors life, and in honoring life it honors death. It also honors the One who made us all with such love. God came to live with us as Jesus, to show us how to live, and to die, and that gives us assurance of the Resurrection, and of life in eternity – beyond time and all that is transient and into God's love forever.

Madeleine L'Engle
Goshen, CT

To the Reader

AS A MAN ON DEATH ROW who several months ago had a date with death, I must confess I had some trepidation at being asked to write down thoughts on this theme. Death was hardly a topic one leaped to embrace. I nodded assent only because of a trust built over hard, long months, and I am glad I did.

This book is a simply but deeply written meditation on that which every living being must face: the ubiquity of death. Here are stories that come from the heart of a self-described "tiny, weak" community that is at the same time – to a man seeking its sweet solace – a very precious pearl.

It is difficult to read the stories without weeping. There's the memory of a mother packing clothes for children she knows she'll be leaving in a few weeks, forever; the agonizing death of a child named Esther; letters of grief

from strangers in prison. There are piercing insights on the social acceptance of euthanasia (in today's thinking, as the book rightly points out, the old have no value – "I needed the bed") contrasted with insights on the joy of children who know only the presence of Love; a poem written by a dying newlywed for her husband.

All in all, the book paints a compelling picture of the power and presence of community, and the endurance of faith in the face of terror, anguish, and loss.

Arnold's memories of civil rights-era state terrorism show us how the original message of Christ finds expression among the poor and the oppressed, not in the armed mania of powerful government. He also demonstrates how the human and divine presence of love can make life worth living, and death less terrifying, a message of deep value in an age when "community" has become a mere synonym for "neighborhood," and death and fear are a part of the national psychosis. And while at first glance the central subject of the book seems to be death, the redeeming core is life: familial, communal life.

This book is a truly moving meditation. Christoph Arnold has told me more than once that he isn't a writer. He is. He writes from his heart and soul.

Mumia Abu-Jamal

Introduction

ARE YOU AFRAID of dying? Have you ever worried about growing old, about becoming a burden to your children? Do you wonder how you would survive the loss of your spouse, a parent, a child? Is someone you love facing illness or death? Whether consciously or subconsciously, every person inevitably faces these questions at one point or another. It is in search of answers to them that I have written this book.

We cannot avoid death. It overshadows all our lives. Epidemics of fatal childhood illness may have almost disappeared in our lifetime, yet among adults heart disease and strokes are more prevalent than ever, and new plagues such as AIDS continue to surface. Despite new and promising treatments, the curse of cancer is still with us. Accidents claim the lives of young and old. Suicide rates have never been higher.

In addition to all this, life has become increasingly cheap. It is not only the gunfire in our streets or random terrorism at airports or in city centers. Our politics are dominated by the fear of death. Every year we squander new resources to further bloat the national defense budget. We build larger, more secure prisons and find new reasons to execute criminals. Yet instead of creating a safer society, we only perpetuate the culture of violence and death.

How and when did we start down this road? Already at the beginning of this century, before Hiroshima and the Holocaust, before even the First World War, the German philosopher Friedrich Nietzsche sounded an alarm. Sensing a catastrophe that no one else seemed to notice, he suggested that society's spiraling descent was directly linked to its abandonment of God:

> Do we not hear the noise of the grave-diggers who are burying God? God is dead! And we have killed him! How shall we console ourselves, the most murderous of all murderers? The holiest and the mightiest has bled to death under our knife – who will wipe the blood from us? With what water could we cleanse ourselves?

Not only is God dead, Nietzsche said; he is no longer relevant. And as the last decades have shown us, one consequence of God's irrelevance is our own. Once we remove God from the picture, we make ourselves and each other irrelevant and redundant. Finally, we isolate ourselves from each other, and then we can kill and be killed without qualms.

It is easier, of course, to pretend that this does not happen. Some go so far as to claim the Holocaust never happened. Others believe the atomic bomb *saved* lives. Yet unless we acknowledge the reality of death's power over our society, we will never be able to free ourselves from its grip. God *is* alive. We must allow him to transform us, and through us our society, so that it is permeated by love, compassion, and justice.

This book is about dying, yes, but the heart of its message is about living. Just as a newborn baby can teach us to fight for life, so can a sickly or aging person. How the newborn struggles for each breath! His determination to live seems even larger than his small body. The same is true of the struggle that often accompanies the end of life. Little by little the lifesap flows away; the flame flickers, and the dying person must concentrate all his energies: just one more breath! In its deepest sense, this twofold fight – at life's beginning, and at its end – mirrors the battle between Satan, the prince of darkness and death, and God, the creator and giver of life.

As elder of the Bruderhof communities (see page 146 below), I have been close to suffering and dying people for many years. It is from this pastoral perspective that I tell the stories of the people who appear in this book. In relating my personal experiences, it is not my intent to lift up the Bruderhof or its members. None of them would have wanted that. In any case, they were all ordinary people like you and me. They had their bad days, their struggles, their low moments. To me their significance lies not so much in the way they died, but in the way they lived.

The people in this book lived life to the full – not for themselves, but for others. In serving a cause greater than themselves, they found the pearl of great price and sold all they had for it. In return they received a sense of purpose and inner direction, courage, and even joy in the face of suffering and death. They lived and strived for the love that, as John says, "casts out fear," and because of this they were able to meet their Maker with peace of heart and mind.

My aim is to point the reader to God. I can assure you, as could all the men and women whose stories are collected here, that in him there is comfort and strength for even the most anxious soul. In him we can find the confidence to say with Paul the Apostle: "O grave, where is your victory? O death, where is your sting?"

J. C. A.

1 Foundations

JUST AS EVERY BUILDING needs a foundation, so each of us needs a strong basis on which to build our life. Many factors in life contribute to building this foundation; the most important, perhaps, is the influence of those who surround us in childhood. The strongest influence on my own life was that of my parents, Heinrich and Annemarie Arnold. Their faith, their prayers, and their devotion to God and to each other through the years formed the cornerstones of my life: my character and my outlook on life and death.

Papa and Mama were God-loving people, but they never used many religious words. Their piety consisted of action – deeds of love to each other, to us children, and to those around them.

Trained as a kindergarten teacher, Mama was also a gifted writer who expressed her deepest thoughts in poems and essays. She was a prolific letter-writer and kept a detailed diary. Mama was always the first one up in the morning and the last to go to bed. Every morning, as we children struggled to get out of bed, she was already busy doing the housework or one of her many other activities – sewing a garment for a new baby, making jelly, or knitting a sweater. She loved swimming and hiking and spent hours tending her flower garden. In summer she would go berry picking even during the hottest midday hours.

Mama never walked anywhere – she ran. Once during a medical emergency, when a baby's life was in danger, it was she who ran for an oxygen tank. She was sixty-three years old at the time, but the man who ran after her to help her carry the tank could not catch up with her. Typically, she never thought of asking anyone else to do it.

Papa, a well-loved pastor and counselor, was a farmer by training. He had studied agriculture in Zurich and run a dairy farm in England for several years. Later, in South America, he worked with horses, transporting food, supplies, and people between three villages. Papa was a tall, strong man. He could lift a 100-lb bag of flour on and off the wagon as if it were nothing. He was also very tender-hearted, especially toward the poor and downtrodden, whom he loved deeply. More than once he returned home from a trip with a tramp who stayed with us for a few days.

Papa had a wonderful sense of humor. When, after years of keeping a clean-shaven chin, he grew a beard, he came downstairs late one evening in his pajamas to tell us that he had a difficult decision to make: should he put his beard under the blankets or on top? Even when he was lying in bed feeling unwell, he would recite poetry to us, often Schiller or Goethe, or reminisce about his boyhood pranks and have us all rocking with laughter. My own children never tired of hearing him tell tales of the Paraguayan jungle and roar like a lion to scare them in fun.

 BENEATH Papa's zest for life, he was a spiritual man with a compassionate heart and a deep love for God. Couples and single men and women from all walks of life confided in him, turning to him with their personal problems for help and advice. In his presence, people were confronted with a spiritual choice: to open up and confess their sins, or to keep them hidden and harden their hearts. Though zealous, even sharp, against sin he always had great compassion for the sinner. He listened to the needs of all who came to him, whether or not they were believers, and carried their burdens with them in prayer. Though this brought him envy from some, it brought genuine trust and love from many others. They knew that Papa was not drawing people to himself, but turning them to the source of real help: to God, to Christ, and to their brothers and sisters.

In 1962, Papa was appointed elder of our church; he humbly served in that capacity until his death twenty years later. Papa trusted his brothers and sisters endlessly.

Despite repeated breaches of trust, he found the courage and humility to forgive those who betrayed or hurt him again and again: "I would rather trust and be betrayed, than live in mistrust." He never tired of preaching forgiveness or pointing out that when people spend their lives harboring grudges, they become crippled by unwittingly binding themselves to the person they cannot forgive. They are imprisoned, yet they refuse to take the key of

forgiveness out of their own pocket and unlock the door.

Papa suffered a great deal in his lifetime. Several times he was gravely ill, almost to the point of death, but miraculously he always pulled through. Mama, who was four years older, was vigorous, active, and hardly ever sick. We children always assumed that Papa would die long before Mama. But God must have had other plans. In the fall of 1979 Mama was found to have cancer of the lymph nodes. Her health deteriorated rapidly, and soon she, who had spent her life serving others, was an invalid who needed to be cared for – a fact she found hard to accept. Yet in spite of her great suffering, she trusted in God and submitted to what she felt was his will for her. She found peace of mind and faced the end without fear.

On the day the doctors informed our family of Mama's sickness, my parents wept, and we wept with them. Then they looked at one another – I will never forget the love in their eyes – and, turning to us children, said, "Now every day, every moment, counts. We must not miss any chance to show our love to our brothers and sisters, to the children, to our guests." Mama told us to trust completely in God's wisdom and leading. It was a heartbreaking but deeply moving moment.

Early in 1980 the deaths of three elderly members of our community – Emmy, Dora, and Ruth – as well as a four-month-old baby, followed one on the other within a two-week period. For more than half a century, all three had been members of our church and close friends of my parents, and their deaths cut deep into Mama's heart. With each passing, she became noticeably weaker. First Papa's mother, our dearly beloved Oma ("grandmother") Emmy, died at the age of ninety-five. It pained Mama that she was not well enough to prepare Oma's body for burial or to set up the room in which she was laid. She had always felt it a privilege to do this last service of love for others who died in our church.

When Dora, whom Mama had known for almost fifty years, passed away only a few days later, I took my parents to see her for the last time. Mama looked at her with unforgettable tenderness, and though she was unable to attend Dora's funeral, she got up from her bed and stood trembling in the doorway as the burial procession passed our house.

Within a week, Ruth, a childhood friend of my father's, died unexpectedly. For her funeral, Mama got dressed and sat up in her bed. It was clearly more than she had strength for, but she insisted on showing her deep love and respect for Ruth.

Children in our community loved Mama and often came to her window to sing. Their childlike trust in her recovery had an immediate effect: when they were there, she became peaceful and radiated joy. Often she said with a sigh, "The children, the children!" She didn't know it, but they met many times in secret to pray for her recovery. Little did Mama know that the weeks of her final illness and her death would play a decisive role for many of them: at that time dozens of them decided to give their lives to Jesus and to follow him. Most of them are now believing men and women with children of their own.

Mama died in March 1980, five months after her illness was diagnosed. Not surprisingly, her death was a heavy blow for my father. They had been married for over forty years and had always worked closely together. Papa had depended heavily on her for her advice. Now he was alone.

Over the next two years Papa's physical strength declined rapidly. He read much in the Bible and still held worship services when he could. In those last years he spoke often about God's ultimate plan for all creation, and emphasized his belief that in the end Jesus will be victorious over all darkness and sin. He said repeatedly:

> My life has become less and less important to me. God's kingdom is what matters. Each of us is so little, so weak. Yet each of us is also an opening for God's love to break into this world. That is what I want to live for; that is worth dying for.

In his last weeks Papa required much care, and different brothers took turns at his bedside each night. Even though he could hardly speak, it was inwardly strengthening just to sit in the room with him. In the final days of his life I spent many hours at his bedside, and I will never forget the powerful sense of the closeness of God.

Papa died peacefully early one morning in the summer of 1982. It was a privilege for me, his only son, to close his eyes forever.

Papa and Mama's lives were firmly grounded in Christ. Their lives were marked by service to others, by trust, and by love. They were outwardly and inwardly fulfilled because they were loyal to their commitments and faithful to their calling.

2 Growth

THE FIRST EVENT of inner significance for my life was a death – the death of my little sister Marianne. Although I was only six when she was born, and I never saw her alive, Marianne's birth and death had a decisive impact on my personal life and my sisters', as well as on my own children years later. Before I was born another sister, Emmy Maria, had also died in infancy. The following poem by my mother, written after Emmy Maria passed away, reveals the depth of Mama's pain, but also her tender love and deep faith.

> You sleep in deep peace on a gentle green hill,
> near to the sky, my child.
>
> The love of your father carried you there
> to a long, long rest in that holy place.
> Sleep, my child.

Enshrined in the earth, the mother of all,
by oneness and love laid to rest.
Sleep, my child.

And when earth awakes and the sun beats down,
its glorious rays will stream on you.
Sleep, my child.

But when the time comes that all is revealed,
when God's Kingdom comes here on earth –
Wake, my child.

Your body will wake from the bosom of earth,
renewed and made free from this world:
Live, my child!

In 1947, when Mama was expecting Marianne, we lived in the Paraguayan backwoods of South America, having been forced to leave Nazi Germany in 1937 and England in 1940. Living conditions were very primitive, also in the small hospital that our church operated. Fortunately three of our members were doctors, and we had several trained nurses and midwives. However, we had very little equipment and medicines; it was before the days of antibiotics, at least in Paraguay.

Just before Marianne's birth, after two days of extremely difficult, life-threatening labor, my mother's heart suddenly stopped beating. The doctors were able to resuscitate her, but both lives were still in very grave danger. My father pleaded with the doctors to perform a Cesarean. The doctor warned him, "Your wife will die if we operate. The only way to save her is to abort the baby; otherwise both mother and baby will be lost." It was a tremendously difficult situation: both my parents believed firmly in the sanctity of all life. Papa went out into the woods to pray.

When he returned, Mama, though she was still in critical condition, had regained consciousness. Then, unexpectedly, the baby was delivered naturally. She had a small bruise on her head from the instruments, but otherwise she seemed healthy. God had intervened.

Yet Mama sensed that not all was well with her child. Marianne did not cry, she did not open her eyes. The next day she quietly died.

Some weeks later Mama wrote to her brother Reinhold in Germany:

> It is so hard to grasp that this child, so greatly longed for, born under such pain, has now left us before we had really got to know her, before we knew what kind of a 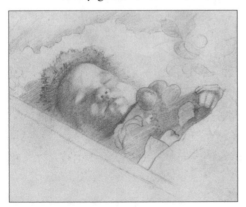 person she would be. Heiner had looked forward so much to having a little baby in his arms again...How glad I was that during the long two-and-a-half days and nights of labor, as also in those hard hours that were so incomprehensible,

my dear Heiner was always at my side, standing by me
so faithfully…

Sometimes it all seems so unreal, like a fleeting, passing dream. But the more we think about it, the more
grateful we feel that the little child was born alive. She
brought great joy, even if only for a few hours, to our
other children, and she led the hearts of people to one
another in love. So the little one really fulfilled a task
on this earth.

No matter how short, every life has a purpose. Papa knew
that, and he thanked God for the rest of his days that he
had not made the decision to abort the baby. It certainly
had far-reaching consequences for our church community,
helping to form our whole attitude to life and death. In
community, life and death can be carried together; that is
the message of the Gospels: "Bear one another's burdens,
and so fulfill the law of Christ" (Gal. 6:2).

ALTHOUGH MARIANNE'S DEATH was important
for me, I remained a very ordinary boy, full of mischief
and frequently in trouble. Like most of the boys I grew up
with, I had a passion for riding horses, going hunting se-
cretly, and watching the gauchos work the cattle and race
their horses. My imagination ran wild with dreams of
being a gaucho one day.

Life was luxuriant in our subtropical paradise, but disease and death lurked around us as well. We saw glimpses
of human misery every day at our mission hospital, where

I often went with Papa to deliver food and supplies. Many of the patients suffered from malnutrition. Leprosy and tuberculosis were prevalent. There were complicated maternity cases, children dying of respiratory ailments, meningitis, or dehydration, and men injured by falling trees or wounded by machetes after drunken brawls.

Papa often told us children about Jesus and how he came for the poor. He told us about men and women through the centuries who gave up everything for the sake of Jesus. One of our favorite stories was that of Vassili Ossipovitch Rachoff, a young Russian aristocrat who left his family and wealth and walked from village to village to help the suffering and dying. I thought about Rachoff long and often.

As a teenager I spent a year away from my family, working as a house boy at our Bruderhof House in Asuncion, the capital of Paraguay. Boys from our church took turns doing this task for several months at a time; it consisted mainly of running errands and doing odd jobs around the house. Often I skipped the Sunday morning service and disappeared into the slums, where I had many friends. Their living conditions were appalling: crowded bamboo shacks with open sewage running between them. The flies and mosquitoes were horrendous. Hundreds of children roamed the streets, many of them orphans, and expert thieves. Some worked as shoe-shiners for the rich – five cents a pair – a job I found so intriguing that I soon got myself a shoe-shine kit and joined them whenever I could.

Bit by bit these children told me about their lives. Many of their parents had either been killed in fights or had died of tropical diseases. They had seen siblings die of illnesses or deficiencies, and they themselves had survived only to continue living in hardship, fear, and danger.

When an unexpected revolution broke out in the city, much of the fighting took place right on our street. We heard the rumble of nearby tanks and machine-gun fire all night. Bullets whizzed over our house. From our windows we saw soldiers being killed. This was war, and at age thirteen, separated from my family, I was scared. What if I were hit?

My great-aunt Monika, who lived in the house with us, noticed how afraid I was and consoled me. A nurse, Monika had served on the front during World War I, and she told me how dying soldiers would lay their heads on her lap and weep like little children in their pain and fear of death; how they cried with remorse for their sins; how they agonized because they would never see their loved ones again. Through her deep faith, Monika had touched them, comforted them, and turned them toward Jesus before they died.

Still, the questions ate at me: Why do people have to die? And why is there so much evil and wickedness in the world? Monika read me the passage from Romans – verses 8:22–27 – about how all creation groans for redemption. She helped me to overcome my fears, especially the fear of death. Like Papa, she told me that somewhere in the universe Christ is preparing a place for us, and I felt it was a very real place, not something abstract. Many times I was reassured by this belief. Finally there was the comfort of those wonderful words of Jesus: "Lo, I am with you always, to the end of the world" (Mt. 28:20).

3 Choices

DAILY, OFTEN HOURLY, we are faced with choices that influence the course of our lives. With choices come the burdens of responsibility and the consequences that result from our decisions. We can choose to be allies of goodness, truth, and godliness, or we can side with evil. As the Christians of the first century put it:

> There are two ways: the one is that of life and the other that of death. There is a great difference between the two ways. The way of life is this: first, you shall love the God who made you; second, you shall love your neighbor as yourself...But the way of death is the way of those who persecute the good and hate the truth, who love lying and do not know the reward of righteousness.[1]

Even a child needs to learn to make conscious decisions for the good: to choose honesty, respect, and friendliness over

lying, arrogance, and bullying. In this regard, my parents'
message to us children was always the same: they stressed
the importance of seeking God's will and then asking him
for the strength to do it.

WHEN MY FAMILY came to the United States in
1955, the Cold War was on, and both superpowers were
carrying out nuclear tests by the dozen and racing each
other to build the most powerful or deadliest weapon. The
horrors of Hiroshima and Nagasaki were still very present,
and the nuclear hysteria that developed was fed by both
the government and the big corporations. Schools had
regular air-raid drills, and families built their own bomb
shelters and stocked them with canned goods. Newspapers
carried stories about possible Soviet attacks on American
cities.

For me, living in the United States was tremendously
exciting – an adventure. At the same time, it was frighten-
ing to be reminded that Woodcrest, our new home, was
within the 90-mile radius that experts predicted would be
doomed if an atomic bomb were ever dropped on New
York City. I never got used to the drills; again and again I
struggled with the fear of bombs and war, and I sensed this
same fear in many of my classmates.

Though I did not do well academically – I had to work
very hard just to get passing grades – I made friends, fell in
love, and was generally very pleased with myself. And even

if I wasn't good at sports, I had chums on the football and track teams.

Soon my friendships and extracurricular activities took the place of my relationship with God. I didn't realize it at the time, but I was living for myself. My life was selfish and empty; it lacked a direction. Then, in my junior year, God stopped me in my tracks. I felt struck in my heart and realized that I was headed the wrong way. I had to make a choice: either to go on drifting and living superficially, or to change and go the way I knew in my heart was God's will for my life. Deep down, I wanted to be close to Jesus, and soon I felt the call to be baptized.

Once I had made up my mind, I spent many hours with my father, telling him everything I could ever remember doing wrong. Papa told me that baptism meant dying to oneself and finding new life in Christ. He also said it demanded commitment. He warned me that fear of commitment is an excuse people often use when they have made an idol of their individual self-fulfillment, and that when they are afraid to commit themselves to something greater, they drift through life. With nothing to live for other than their own desires – no real cause or goal – their lives remain empty. He told me that if I really wanted to be baptized, I had to be willing to give up *everything* for Jesus. I felt I was ready to do this, and I was baptized. I will never forget that experience, especially the overwhelming joy of having a clear conscience.

LIKE BAPTISM, the Civil Rights Movement of the
1960s called me – as countless others – to choose whether
or not I would stand up for what I knew was right on the
question of racism. Martin Luther King was an inspiring
figure for me in those days. His belief in the cause of
justice was unwavering, and he seemed utterly fearless,
though he surely knew he would be killed for his efforts.
Only a few days before his assassination, in 1968, he said:

> Like anybody, I would like to live a long life. Longevity
> has its place. But I'm not concerned about that now.
> I just want to do God's will. And He's allowed me to
> go up to the mountain. And I've looked over. And I've
> *seen* the Promised Land. And I may not get there with
> you. But I want you to know tonight that we as a
> people *will* get to the Promised Land! So I'm happy
> tonight. I'm not worried about *anything*. I am not
> fearing *any* man. Mine eyes have seen the glory of the
> coming of the Lord![2]

To me, King's life carried an important message. Already
several years earlier our church had taken up the challenge
of his vision of racial harmony and joined in the struggle
in the South. How could we stand by and still call ourselves a church?

In 1965, a friend and I traveled to Alabama. It was just
three weeks before the now-famous Selma march, and
tensions were rising. Once there we heard of the murder
of Jimmie Lee Jackson, a young black who was severely
beaten on the head and shot in the stomach by white

police while attempting to register to vote. He died a week later.

Shaken and horrified, and wanting to stand with these persecuted and oppressed people in their suffering, we decided to attend Jimmie Lee's memorial service. What we experienced there was remarkable and unforgettable: despite continuing hatred against the city's black community, there was not a note of anger or revenge in the chapel. On the contrary, there was a palpable spirit of courage and hope, expressed in songs like "We shall overcome" and "Free at last." Martin Luther King was present; he urged us all to continue in the way of nonviolence and to forgive the police.

The stark contrast of the atmosphere we met on leaving the church only strengthened our solidarity with King's movement: lined up across the street stood state troopers armed with nightsticks. Under their hateful stares, and followed by the insults of local policemen and white supremacists, we marched to the cemetery.

Jimmie Lee had made a choice and paid the ultimate price for it. For us, and for the many other "outside agitators" who went to Selma at that time, the choices we made were also not without danger. After the funeral, we drove three black women back to Selma; only days later a white woman with black passengers was shot and killed near Montgomery.

Selma taught me a lesson I have never forgotten: that the redemptive power of love and forgiveness is the only answer to hatred. Yet many times since then I had to ask myself: Would I have responded the way those black people did?

4 Despair

THE DEMON OF DESPAIR lurks at the edge of every human heart. Each of us has experienced its chilling touch. Who has not suffered anguish of mind at one point or another, to the point of sleepless nights, because of some burden, some guilt, some gnawing need? Emotional ups and downs are part of human life, but when discouragement grows and turns to hopelessness it often seems insurmountable. At times like these we are in danger of despair.

Despair is one of our greatest enemies. It means the loss of all joy, all hope, all confidence – sometimes even the will to live. To be sure, feelings of inadequacy and worthlessness are normal. There are times when we feel we are not worthy of love or friendship but, like Kafka's beetle, insects worthy to be squashed. Yet despair can be deeper than this, and, at least in my experience, I have sensed that self-centeredness often lies at its core.

Many people spend their lives in darkness, ruled by a sense of guilt. Sooner or later, self-accusation tempts them to self-destruction. Suicide is more common today than ever before. Many elderly people see it as a simple solution to their complex problems: to loneliness due to the death of spouse or friends, to the loss of control and independence, to feelings of uselessness and vulnerability. They fear being a burden to their families; they fear emotional or physical pain. Perhaps most important, they fear a long-drawn-out dying.

Driven as they are by the pressures of our success-oriented society, thousands of otherwise capable people are trapped into believing that suicide is a way out. Adolescents and young adults are at particular risk, mostly because they fear failure and rejection. Small wonder that many see no purpose in living. As Pascal pointed out long ago, knowledge of our misery without knowledge of God leads to despair. He also said that knowledge of God without knowledge of our misery leaves us sick with arrogance and pride. Where there is no faith in God, the right fear of God is lacking, and then the whole foundation of human morality wavers.

Many who attempt suicide do not really want to die. Their desperation is a cry for attention, a cry for help. It must not be ignored, but taken seriously. One unsuccessful attempt is often followed by another. Without help and intervention, it will only be a matter of time before it succeeds

IN THE 1970s my father brought home a homeless alcoholic named Terry. He was thirty-two years old, and a Vietnam veteran. As a child he had been sexually abused, and the terrible memories of his childhood often pulled him into deep depression. Papa spent much time with him, listening to him, counseling him, and simply being his friend. He also arranged for him to receive psychiatric help and medication. Everyone loved Terry, and he stayed with us for more than a year.

Then one day Terry left us, haunted by the demons of his past. Soon afterward we heard that he had killed himself. It was a tremendous shock, especially to my father, who had loved Terry dearly. It was as if a beloved family member had died. He wept for Terry, and he wept for the need and sin of the whole world.

One could almost say that it was futile to try to help a man like Terry; that he didn't have a chance. Yet I have experienced over and over again that people *can* receive healing from their past and be protected from suicidal temptation.

Over the past decades many desperate people have turned to me for pastoral help. Often their personal lives were in turmoil, and anguish over relationships, family members, jobs, or money matters had upset the delicate balance of their emotions. Sometimes guilt and unconfessed sin were at the root of their depression and suicidal thoughts. In other cases there was simply no rational explanation to be found.

No one knows why certain people struggle through life with tormenting thoughts and temptations. Some may just have a depressive tendency; they may be predisposed to depression and suicide. Medication is often helpful, and professional help may be sought, but in the end the despairing person must *want* help. He must be willing to open his heart to someone he trusts.

If he takes his situation into his own hands, he forfeits the possibility of help, human or divine. Every person needs a trusting relationship with someone with whom he can share his deepest troubles: a minister, priest, rabbi, or a close friend. Talking things out and confessing our sins can bring remarkable freeing to the soul and change a person's whole attitude to life.

Ultimately hope and healing will not come through our own efforts. We cannot isolate ourselves in our need. God created us as communal beings. If our minds and hearts are engaged in active community with others, we will find help in our despair. The truly communal person, no matter how despairing, can find peace. But it will require complete trust – both to man and to God.

Every person, believing or not, must acknowledge the power of evil. It is the work of the devil, whom the Bible calls "the Accuser" and "the murderer from the beginning." As a force of evil, Satan is not abstract; he is very real. He knows our weakest points and strikes directly at the soul, using every means, including mental illness, to break us down. He throws people into deep despair and depression, into a dark heaviness that may not lift for years. In other instances he causes people to accuse themselves, to exaggerate rather unremarkable weaknesses and vices and turn them into seemingly insurmountable walls.

No one is wholly at the mercy of the power of evil. Far more often we are at the mercy of ourselves. Often it is pride and unrepented sin that separate us from God. He waits for us to come to him, like children to a wise and loving father. If we go to him and to our brothers and sisters to confess our sins, we will experience the powerful redemption of an unburdened conscience.

No sin, no guilt, is beyond forgiveness. The Bible tells us about the woman caught in adultery who was brought before Jesus. He told her accusers they could stone her to death, but added that he who was without sin should throw the first stone. They all left, one by one. Then Jesus said these amazing words: "Woman, neither do I accuse you. Go now and sin no more" (Jn. 8:11). It was as simple as that.

Christ condemns the sin, but not the sinner. His love for us is so much greater, his compassion so much broader, than ours for one another. And he said that he came not for the healthy or the righteous, but for the sick and the sinners (Lk. 5:32).

There is help. There is hope. There is healing for the despairing soul. God, in his love to each one of us, sent us his Son, who wants to free us from our past, our sins, our burdens. He promises us, "Come to me, all who are heavy laden, and I will give you rest. Take my yoke upon you, and learn from me; for I am gentle and lowly in heart, and you will find rest for your souls" (Mt. 11:28–29).

5 The Spiritual Battle

IN THE NEW TESTAMENT we read of the powers and principalities that battle over the earth in a continuous struggle between the spirit of life and love and the spirit of death and darkness. I am not referring to the current obsession with the occult; I am speaking of the ever-present struggle between good and evil, which, though invisible, is nonetheless a reality. The person who is truly in touch with God will be aware of this spiritual battle. Only modern man, in his arrogance and so-called objectivity, has begun to doubt the reality of the power of evil.

This fight is particularly intense where an individual soul is at stake. Some people are especially vulnerable, beset with spiritual fears, and may have to cope with disabling anxieties throughout their whole lives. I want to encourage all who know fear, but I have on my heart especially those in whom this fear is an overwhelming personal struggle.

We live in a time when there is every reason to be anxious and afraid, but we do have a loving God who has his hand over us. If only we could believe this, we would find peace, and our fears would be laid to rest. Hardship or suffering may still be a part of our lives, but we must believe that God will give us the strength to face it.

Dorie Came to the Bruderhof in 1953, seeking inner peace and looking for something worthwhile to live for. Soon she became part of our family, a big sister to us children. After my parents died, she joined my own family and lived with us in our home.

The Dorie most people knew was a happy person who found great joy in helping and serving others. When a baby was born she cleaned the house, brought fruit and flowers, and made everything ready for mother and baby's homecoming. When guests were expected she made sure the room was swept and dusted, the beds freshly made, a bouquet on the table. She was cheerfully willing to do the smallest deed of love for anyone, and she never expected or wanted thanks.

Underneath, however, Dorie was a nervous, anxious person. All her life she struggled with fear. She had trouble sleeping at night and always wanted to have someone near by. She dreaded getting older; she feared physical ailments and possible disability. She was afraid of cancer, afraid of dying. Yet because her determination to live for others filled her mind and heart, she was able to keep in check the worries that would have otherwise preoccupied her entirely or driven her to the brink.

Then cancer struck. For six years Dorie battled it bravely. Initially she underwent several months of chemotherapy. Each session found her so apprehensive, so distraught, that she required continual inner and emotional support. One sensed it was not just a matter of ordinary human anxiety, but a vital fight for her soul and spirit.

Then came a four-year remission, and then a relapse. Dorie's determination to live gave her strength for another round of therapy, and she was granted two more years. But then the cancer recurred again. This time it grew rapidly, and we knew her time on earth was limited. Dorie was in severe pain, and radiation provided only partial relief. With her, my wife and I sought for answers to her questions: What is death? Why do we have to die? Is there life after death? Together we read many passages from Scripture about death and resurrection, and searched for verses that would encourage her. Talking about the moment of death itself, we shared our belief that it simply means being called home to God, and that there is nothing to be afraid of if we have lived an upright life. We assured her that she had served God during her life, and that he would reward her.

The last weeks of Dorie's life were an enormous struggle, both physically and spiritually. She seemed besieged by dark powers. Once she cried out that something evil had entered her room. With what little strength she had, she threw a pillow at it, shouting, "Go away, darkness! Go away!" Again, we felt this was not just a mental state, but a spiritual battle over her soul. At such times we would all gather around her and turn to God with song or prayer. Dorie loved the Lord's Prayer very much; it was always an encouragement to her. My wife and daughters nursed her night and day and accompanied her through many hours of inner torment. Her fortitude made it a privilege for them to care for her.

One morning, after a particularly hard night, Dorie's fear was suddenly gone, and she said, "I want to depend on God alone." There was only joy and anticipation of that great moment when he would call her home. She felt it would be very soon. When I visited her, she told me: "There's a surprise today: the kingdom's coming! When it comes, I will run downstairs and outside to welcome it!" That same afternoon she exclaimed, "All the pain is gone. I feel better! Thank you, thank you, God!" A little later she said with a smile, "God will call me home tonight." In the evening she called our family together and hugged each one of us in farewell. We sang and prayed by her bed through the night. She was completely peaceful. As dawn was breaking she slipped away from us.

The Bible speaks in several places of the great battle in the universe, but when I think of Dorie, two stories in particular come to mind. One is the book of Daniel (chapter 10), where we read of an angel who could not gain access to Daniel because of evil spirits blocking the way. (Eventually the archangel Michael was able to break through the barrier.) The other is the Letter of Jude (1:9), in which Michael disputes with the devil over Moses' soul and body. Dorie felt the conflict between good and evil throughout her life, and it caused her great need, but she clung to God and allowed him to guide her. At the end, surrounded by a gathered church who carried her needs with her and interceded for her in prayer, she experienced victory.

6 Reverence

THE BIRTH of a baby is one of the greatest miracles of creation. After many months of waiting and hours of painful labor, a new being comes into the world. Since time began, it has been celebrated with great joy as a gift from God: "When a woman is in travail, she has sorrow, because her hour has come; but when she is delivered of the child, she no longer remembers the anguish, for joy that a child is born into the world" (Jn. 16:21). Yet there is wisdom in the old saying that a woman in labor has one foot in the grave: even in our day, every birth is attended by some anxiety, and there is always the chance of something going mortally wrong.

The death of an infant, the birth of a stillborn baby, or the experience of a miscarriage is not only a painful event but a particularly hard test of our faith. One wonders, "Why did God create a child at all, if it was to live so briefly?" The thought that perhaps its brief sojourn here on earth carries a message from God's kingdom is an awe-inspiring one, but it does not necessarily lessen a parent's grief. Clearly we stand before a mystery that only God understands, and all we can do is hold it reverently in our hearts.

Leo Tolstoy, the great 19th-century Russian novelist, wrote the following after the death of one of his own children:

> How often have I asked myself, and many ask them-selves, "Why do children die?" And I never found an answer. But just recently, when I wasn't thinking about children at all any more...I became convinced that the only task in the life of each individual consists in strengthening love in himself, and in doing that, trans-mitting it to others and strengthening love in them also.
>
> Our child lived so that those of us who were around him would be inspired by the same love; so that in leav-ing us and going home to God, who is Love itself, we are drawn all the closer to each other. My wife and I were never so close to each other as now, and we never before felt in ourselves such a need for love, nor such an aversion to any discord or any evil. [3]

Unfortunately, the love and reverence Tolstoy describes are rare, if not almost completely absent, in our day and age. Below, Doug and Ruby Moody, longtime members of our Bruderhof community, share their story:

WHEN DAVID, our first child, was born in 1944 we had no idea of our Rh incompatibility. David was a healthy baby. Several years later, our second child, Ann Elizabeth, was born. When Ruby's labor pains began, we walked the mile to the clinic; some time later we were rejoicing in the wonder of the birth of a beautiful baby girl.

At delivery the doctor had noticed something wrong and was worried, but he did not indicate this to us. We spent the night in unshadowed joy with our new daughter. In the morning we heard that the doctor was very concerned for the baby. We had to take her to a hospital halfway across the state, but since the birth had not taken place at that hospital, Ruby was not allowed to stay with the baby. We had to return home. Waiting for news was agonizing. The hours seemed endless, but we could do nothing. We had no direct contact with the hospital.

On the second day, our precious little daughter's life was snuffed out. Ruby was inconsolable and wept and wept. It only increased our pain when the doctors told us the problem and implied that there was little hope, medically seen, for us to have any more living children.

Leaving Ruby at home, I drove out alone to bring the little body back to be buried. On arrival at the hospital, however, I was informed that the body of the baby had been turned over to a local undertaker, as required by state law.

At the funeral home I was at first received with great courtesy and solicitude. But when the undertaker realized I was not there to buy a casket or arrange a funeral, he became icy and left the room. I waited at the front desk with the baby's bassinet. When he returned with our little girl, he was holding her upside down by the feet, with one hand. I pulled back the quilt, one Ruby had made for our baby, but before I could do more, the man dropped her into the bassinet. He was cold, disgusted.

On the long, lonely drive home, I had to fight very hard to find forgiveness in my heart for the undertaker. I prepared a grave on our homestead, and together we  laid our little girl to rest with very sore hearts.

Later, after we joined the Bruderhof, we lost another little child, but this second experience was indescribably different. It was redeeming. After our initial shock at the death, we were helped to overcome our deep pain in the loving embrace of the church, and with the faith that there is victory over the powers of death. As someone said to us at the time, no life – and no hope for life – is ever in vain. We were immersed in an atmosphere of reverence.

Our age lacks reverence. How often we treat each other callously! We deny each other basic human rights, we leave basic needs unmet. Irreverence characterizes our thinking, our talk, our actions.

Reverence is awe and gratefulness for what God has made. It is respect for life. Without it, the soul sickens. We must protect reverence like an eternal flame, for without it, our love will remain only an abstract ideal. Reverence is the essence of compassion.

7 When a Baby Dies

EVERY MOTHER KNOWS the quickening of heartbeat, the awful, cold panic that grips her when she fears for her child. When Judy bent over to pick up Dwayne from his crib one day in November, 1973, she found him ashen, without breath. She cried out in shock. Sisters came running; nurses and a doctor were called. Oxygen was brought, and resuscitation efforts started. But an hour later we had to accept the fact that Dwayne was gone from us.

Dwayne was not quite three months old. He had been a happy baby, crying only when hungry or tired. He loved his bath and fussed when it was over. Like all healthy infants he slept a lot, but when he was awake he was alert, and cooed and smiled.

The day had started like any other. Only a short while before, Dwayne had been asleep, breathing normally. I was

away from home when my wife Verena called me with the shaking news of Dwayne's death. I returned at once. Soon our whole community was gathered. We spoke words of comfort to the parents, sang songs, and prayed that Dwayne's parents might be assured that he was with God; we asked that God be close to them in the pain of their loss. We had all suffered a great shock, and we all felt in need of comfort.

A few days later, a sister in one of our communities wrote to Dwayne's parents:

> If you have ever lost a baby, then you always have a baby. Your other children grow up and leave you, but the baby you have lost is always your baby. At life's end, you will have a precious baby waiting for you at the gates of eternity.

Dwayne's death was a shattering experience for us all. We wanted to place complete trust and faith in God, yet we were sick with worry. It was not the first time we had lost a little one to what is now called Sudden Infant Death Syndrome. On the other hand, we felt we could not live in fear, but had to remember that God gives each child a guardian angel to watch over him night and day.

The following words by a mother express the tension many felt at the time:

> No sooner had our dear little baby been born and I loved him so, than I thought of the horror of losing him. Life used to seem so safe, and now it seems so transient and unsafe. If I did not believe in the eternal love of Jesus and the miracle that will bring in the deathless kingdom of God, I think I should go insane.

EACH TIME A BABY or small child dies, we are reminded that the earth is not yet fully our home and that our life here is short – like a flower, like grass, like a butterfly. No matter how young the child, no matter how many hours or days or months we were given to love and know that child, the pain seems unendurable; the wounds never quite seem to heal. What else can we do but trust, with the grieving parents, that in Jesus healing *will* be given, even though slowly and almost imperceptibly?

In a newborn child we see innocence and perfection, and we look for the day when the whole universe will be redeemed and all creation made perfect again, the day when there will be no more death. We believe – the Bible assures us of it – that this will happen when Christ comes again. Writer George Macdonald, who lost children of his own, once wrote:

If the very hairs of our head are all numbered, and He said so who knew, our children do not drop haphazard into this world, neither are they kept in it by any care or any power of medicine; all goes by heavenliest will and loveliest ordinance. Some of us will have to be ashamed of our outcry for our dead.

Beloved, even for your dear faces we can wait awhile, seeing it is His Father, your Father, our Father, to whom you have gone. Our day will come, and your joy and ours, and all shall be well.[4]

8 The Childlike Spirit

RACHEL AND HER MOTHER Mari were making toffee in a pot over an open fire (the only means of cooking in our Paraguayan communities, even in 1958) when Mari was called away "only for a moment." Just then nine-year-old Rachel bent over to stir the candy, and her apron caught fire. She screamed and ran for help, her other clothes bursting into flame. Her father Jack heard her cries and came running. He rolled her on the ground, quickly extinguishing the flames, but the damage was done: one-fourth of her body was severely burned.

Brought directly to our mission hospital, Rachel was given the best of care, but by the next day her condition had worsened. Our doctors used a radio to consult with a specialist in Asuncion, the nearest city, but she continued to go downhill and, despite morphine, to suffer intense pain. Yet she was a brave child. In her innocence, she asked

no questions and remained free of the anxieties that might have burdened an older mind. Fluid loss from her burns depleted her strength, however, and by evening of the fourth day she was not responsive. Her family sat by her bed, singing the songs they knew she loved. At one point her mother called to her to speak once more, and quite unexpectedly she sat upright and sang a few lines with them, until her breathing became labored. Minutes later, she passed away.

In the days that followed, her family remembered that some time before the accident, Rachel had tidied up or given away her few belongings. Only one week before, she had also talked with her mother about death – they were sitting out under the stars – partly in response to the news of another child's death (someone she did not know) but mostly, it seemed, out of her yearning to know more about God. Perhaps she was intuitively preparing for her own parting.

ESTHER MARIE, another girl who died several decades later, bore her suffering and dying in the same spirit of childlike faith. She was a lively girl who enjoyed hiking,

cycling, swimming, and running games. In December, 1982, her left knee began to hurt. It appeared to be a bruise from a recent tumble while sledding, but over the next weeks it only became worse. Then X-rays revealed cancer of the bone just above the knee.

Esther's mother, Johanna, had died of a sudden brain hemorrhage after the birth of a little sister when Esther was four. Johanna had once said to her husband, David, "If I should die, Esther is the one who would miss me the most." Her words proved to be true. All the same, when David married my sister Roswith some years later, Esther accepted her new mother lovingly and found healing.

At the children's hospital where my wife and I had accompanied Esther and her parents, it was decided not to put her through an experimental chemotherapy course that offered less chance for cure than the standard treatment, amputation at the thigh. It was a very hard decision to make, but we hoped Esther would learn to use a prosthesis and live a normal life. When the surgeon told Esther about the amputation, her acceptance of the matter was heartbreaking. There was no rebellion; instead, she replied with a simple, heartfelt "Thank you!" – a trusting response that completely disarmed the doctor. Later she wept, but she listened when we reminded her of the angels who were watching over her.

Once back at home and fully recovered from the surgery, Esther took up life eagerly again, mastering her crutches, skillfully maneuvering her hand-driven tricycle, practicing the piano. A few weeks later she was fitted with the prosthetic leg. Learning to use it was hard work; it meant therapy every day, and sometimes she grew discouraged. One morning she cried, thinking she would never learn to walk again. But later the same day she said, "Look, shall I show you something?" And then she walked – by herself, without crutches. It was only a few steps, but it was a beginning, and she was very pleased.

In early July, the prosthetist had Esther walk up and down in his office for three hours while he made the necessary adjustments. She never complained, although she was obviously tired. Just as he was finishing, she started to vomit. Suddenly she had a seizure. Rushed by ambulance to the nearest hospital, she was given various tests all night, and had several more seizures. Nothing seemed to make sense.

When the test results came, they showed that Esther's cancer had spread to her heart and was causing her seizures. Immediate surgery was necessary, though very risky. Our communities were called together to pray for her survival. At one point during the operation her heart stopped, and the surgeon feared she would suffer brain damage.

Only days before, Esther had seemed to be doing so well. Now she lay comatose, her life hanging on a thread. We decided to bring her home as soon as possible. As we carried her into her room, we wondered if she would be able to leave it again. All we could do was put all our trust in God: he would heal her or take her to himself.

Then came the morning about ten days later when a faint smile played over her face as her mother kissed her. She was waking up from her coma! Her younger brothers and sisters came in. She opened her eyes a little and looked at them, and began to cry. On the one hand, it seemed as if she could not see, as if she was looking past this world into eternity; on the other, her gaze was so penetrating and intense, we wondered what she saw.

The next weeks brought many visitors. Her friends came often, and though she could not always respond, she made distinct efforts to speak. Her speech was garbled at first, but she kept trying, and one morning as her mother was sitting on the edge of the bed, Esther pushed with her leg. "I am going to get out of bed and walk." She was even beginning to joke and tease again. It seemed that she was being given back to us. Still, the atmosphere around her seemed to be other-worldly. She could not tolerate quarreling among her brothers and sisters, and she became the family peacemaker whenever arguments broke out.

Although it cost her unbelievable effort, Esther was

determined to spend as much time as she could with her friends, and she often went out with them in her wheelchair. She was almost blind; she could no longer recognize faces or read. She couldn't control her hands properly (when she tried to clap, her hands totally missed each other), and she needed help with eating. Yet she was certain she would regain what she had lost, and trusted in full recovery: "Daddy, I think that by Christmas I'll be able to walk again. I might need a cane, but I will walk!"

Only days later, early in the morning, my wife and I were unexpectedly called to the house. Esther was taking slow, gasping breaths, and her pulse could no longer be found. She was starting her upward journey. A big tear rolled slowly down her cheek, as if in farewell. As we prayed for the protection of her soul, she took her last breath.

> We give them back to you, dear Lord,
> Who gavest them to us.
> Yet as thou didst not lose them in giving,
> So we have not lost them by their return.
> For what is thine is ours always, if we are thine.
> And life is eternal and love is immortal,
> And death is only a horizon,
> And a horizon is nothing more
> Than the limit of our sight.
>
> *Quaker prayer*

For most of a year, Esther had suffered intensely. Yet remarkably, the more she suffered, the more she trusted; the more she endured, the more thankful she became. Her short life was a fulfilled one, perhaps more fulfilled than the lives of many of us who have lived decades longer. It touched all kinds of people – not only our community, but doctors, hospital staff, even men and women in prison. Some of Esther's classmates were corresponding with prison inmates at the time and had told them her story. One woman wrote from Alabama:

> Lord, how I wish I could help. If I could just come and hold her hand and pray for her my heart would feel better. I'm a mother too, you know. It could be my daughter.

Another prisoner wrote:

> I didn't show any emotion when I was found guilty or when I was given the death penalty, and I was wondering if I had any feelings inside anymore. I found that out when I read your letter. I didn't know the little girl, but I cried as if she was my own daughter. She was that special, my heart was heavy for several days and I prayed for her.
>
> Yesterday my dad came to see me. I hadn't seen my dad since I was one-and-a-half years old, and I've always wondered how I would feel to see the man that walked out on us. We cried and told each other that we love each other. I know I could never have done that without Esther coming into my life first and breaking my wall.

9 Courage

I HAVE OFTEN FELT that we who call ourselves Christians would do well to read about the early believers and how they faced death. Despite persecution those first followers of Jesus remained not only faithful to his teachings, but triumphant, courageous, and joyful. They understood that God's judgment must come over the earth before something new could be created; they knew that death must precede resurrection, and they were not afraid. If we want to be his disciples, we too must be ready to endure suffering and death.

The witness of the first martyrs to the power of faith in Christ, even at the hour of death, still radiates today, as do these words of Polycarp, who died in 156 A.D.:

"Eighty-six years have I served him, and he has never done me any harm. How could I blaspheme my king and savior? You threaten me with a fire that burns for an hour and goes out after a short time, for you do not know the fire of the coming judgment and of eternal punishment for the godless. Why do you wait? Bring on whatever you will."

As Polycarp spoke these and similar words, he was full of courage and joy. His face shone with inward light. He was not in the least disconcerted by all their threats. The proconsul was astounded. Three times he sent his herald to announce in the midst of the arena, "Polycarp has confessed that he is a Christian!"

Now everything happened much faster than it can be told. The mob rushed to collect logs and brushwood…The fuel for the pyre was very quickly piled around him. When they wanted to fasten him with nails, he refused. "Let me be. He who gives me the strength to endure the fire will also give me the strength to remain at the stake unflinching, without the security of your nails."[5]

Like Polycarp, hundreds, perhaps thousands, of the first Christians suffered death for their conviction. Yet they seemed to be strangers to fear. When one of them died, they felt he or she was simply moving from one place to another. For them the world was only a bridge: "Cross over it, but do not build your house on it."[6]

IN OUR OWN TIME we can still find the courage of the earliest believers here and there in people who have submitted their lives to God's will. I will never forget Lynn, a member of our Bruderhof communities who was diagnosed with leukemia in 1979, just after her sixth child was born. At first, chemotherapy and radiation put her cancer into remission; soon, however, it returned. Lynn knew her life might be very short, yet she was not afraid. Quite consciously and willingly she prepared to leave this life and enter the next.

More often than not, the strain of illness taxes individuals and relationships; in Lynn's case, her cancer brought about a transformation in her character, and she became a new person – rather than irritating her, it seemed to make her joyful, outgoing, and tenderhearted.

When her leukemia flared a third time, Lynn's specialists urged her to consider experimental treatment at a distant hospital, even though it would mean being away from her husband James, their children, and the church. Feeling that such treatment held out a false hope, Lynn decided to forgo the treatment: might it not amount to a human grasping to prolong life – something that to them clearly seemed to counter God's will? James and Lynn believed that God had their family in his hand, and this gave them courage to entrust the future to him. She wrote:

> We long to be welded heart to heart and soul to soul like a ring – with no beginning and no end, no greatness and no smallness among us. But this comes only from being completely and firmly grounded and centered in Jesus and his cross. More and more I see how each day I must take up that cross for myself.

Knowing she probably had little time left, Lynn used her

last energy to prepare for the future of her children. She
saw to getting bigger beds for them and extending their
quilts to fit; she made them each a photo album and a
special baby outfit for each one to keep for his or her own
family some day. In consideration of whoever might care
for them after she was gone, she put their clothing and
belongings in order. Beyond that, Lynn poured out her
love to friends and neighbors, and she prepared herself in
an inner way for the hour of death. As my father said at
the time, she was like one of the five wise virgins preparing
to meet the Bridegroom.

As Lynn's strength waned, she was less and less able to
spend time in the family living room; whenever she did,

however, she was there fully, listening to the children tell of the day's activities, settling a quarrel, or reading a story. Even when nausea confined her to bed, she did not relinquish her role as mother; she took as much time as possible with each child, in addition to responding to visitors. At the end she could only reach out with her eyes. Lynn died at home, in her own bed, surrounded by her family.

Why a young mother like Lynn should be stricken with such an illness and taken from her family will always remain a mystery. There is no simple answer – only the choice between rebelling at the burden, or accepting it in faith. Lynn and her husband had faith and through this found unquestioning trust in God, and it gave them both incredible courage as they faced eternity. With the same conviction and joy of the early Christians, Lynn did not cringe from death but devoted herself fully to living life for God until he took her to himself.

10 Readiness

WHEN WE LOSE A LOVED ONE our first instinct is to protest, and that is only natural. God's original plan did not include suffering and death; only through Adam and Eve's disobedience did these become reality.

Xaverie, an energetic, cheerful woman, was a devoted wife and mother. Her illness came in the prime of life – she was thirty-three – and it struck suddenly, just two weeks after the birth of her second child, Gareth. First her eyes ached, then she had stomach pains, then lumps on her scalp. She started the week on Tylenol and ended it on morphine. By the middle of the next she was gone.

When Xaverie was told she had cancer, she was almost awed by it. To her husband John she said, "Well, God does not ask us to carry more than we can bear, so he must feel that I can carry this." And to her mother: "You know, my greatest fear in life was that I would get cancer. Yet the

minute I heard I had it, I had absolutely no fear."

Later her mother, Sibyl, wrote,

> When we heard of the diagnosis, she said, "John, Mama, I want no long faces, no tears. I don't want this to be a big holy experience. I want it to be a joyful, childlike one, like Merrill's." [Merrill was a close friend who had died of cancer the year before.] I gulped inwardly, and possibly John did too. How in the world were we going to put this brave face on? But her response showed me the importance of the witness of each brother and sister; she had had a powerful role model in Merrill.

Xaverie saw her illness as a call to give up her love of life and her family for the greater love of God, and her years of daily surrender to Christ gave her strength to make this new, greater sacrifice. Naturally she loved her children dearly, as any mother would, but she knew she now had another task, and she did not cling to them emotionally. She was even thankful when another woman came to care for them.

Incredibly, never once during those quick, few weeks of sickness and dying did she express any anxiety about the future, about life after death. She simply entrusted John and her children to the church. No one heard her breathe a word of complaint or saw her shed a tear.

One day when Verena and I came to see her, she asked for the laying on of hands. A few days later we held a service to do this. Xaverie was brought in on a wheeled stretcher, with an intravenous line and oxygen. As she entered the room, she tried to sit up, and waved cheerfully. In a photo that captured this moment, one can see the anguish on her husband's face – on Xaverie's, however, there is none. Her face is shining with expectancy and joy. Certain that she could be healed if that was God's plan, she was also completely ready to die. As I laid my hands on her, she looked at me trustingly and said, "With God, everything is possible!" The gathering was quietly hopeful, yet it was also heartrending. Everyone in the room was shaken, and there were many tears. We all felt the presence of eternity in our midst.

The next morning Verena and I visited her again, and I said, "Xaverie, we trust in God's will for you. Are you ready for eternity?" She assured us that nothing burdened her conscience, and that she was at peace: "I will accept God's will, whatever it is. I am ready." In the evening of the same day she died.

Although most of us did not know it at the time, Xaverie's death deeply touched another dying person – a young man with AIDS from San Francisco who was visiting the Bruderhof "to say good-bye." Bob had grown up in a conservative congregation in Ohio, but as a young man he had rebelled against his upbringing, moving first to Paris and then to California, where he led an actively gay lifestyle. When Bob realized that his life was going to be cut short, he sought community with the church of his youth; sadly, the congregation missed an opportunity to reach out and instead rejected him as someone who had committed an "unpardonable" sin. Xaverie's courage in meeting death – and the compassion Bob felt at the Bruderhof, which he had come to know some time before, on another visit – gave him strength to face his own terminal illness.

Only a few months later, Bob died. Like Xaverie, he was in his thirties; like her, he met death with the knowledge that it can be a beginning as well as an end.

RILLA, A SINGLE WOMAN of thirty-five, died of skin cancer. She had undergone surgery two years earlier, but as soon as she realized that there was no further medical help

available, she came to the conviction that there was nothing accidental about the recurrence of the disease, and she accepted it. Every aspect of it, she felt, including its timing, was God's will.

Rilla was a tall, red-haired woman with a radiant smile – a person you could not forget. Soft-spoken but not reserved, she loved the beautiful things in life: flowers, music, poetry, children. Her social conscience, sharpened by the civil rights struggle of the 1960s, gave her an unyielding concern for the poor, the elderly, the disabled. She felt continually torn between her desire to help the underprivileged and the marginalized of society, and the call she felt to join hands with our Bruderhofs, where we have sought to build up communities in which there are no underprivileged or marginalized people.

Rilla's cancer was diagnosed when my father was on his deathbed, and it was the first time that Verena and I supported a dying person without my father's advice and counsel, something I had always depended on.

A torn, rather complicated person, Rilla was often distressed about her own weaknesses; she had struggled for years to find faith. Through the experience of Papa's last days, however, and the realization of her own impending death, life suddenly became simple for her. Rilla asked me to baptize her, and I did this one week after Papa's death. The transformation and healing given to Rilla through her newly-strengthened faith was remarkable. She said, "I am experiencing God's grace in my life; the richness and fullness of God! It can't be measured in months or days; God's time isn't measured in our way."

As Rilla's illness progressed, she felt the urgency of using each day to the full. There was much she wanted to accomplish and put in order while she still had strength. Often, she expressed her deepest thoughts in poetry, as in these lines written when my mother was dying, also of cancer, two years before:

> Behind you we stand at the doorway to eternity
> Looking out onto what we do not know –
> Onto God's ocean of stars.
> Come, take my hand,
> For you must enter this dark house
> And find your way through its grim passages...
> But even here, in this dark place,
> Small lights are kindled,
> Points of radiant love...

When Rilla went through her poetry collection with her brother Justin and told him who should get each piece, he was taken aback by her carefree anticipation of her passing. The next morning she said she was sorry that she had burdened him by talking about death; she did not want to add to his pain.

Again and again Rilla would turn the conversation to the needs of others. She wished to visit people who were sick, even though these visits exhausted her. She wept for the need of the world, especially for the suffering of children, saying, "Our hearts are so small, but we can still wish that they are somehow stretched wider, to pray for all who suffer."

Neither Rilla nor Xaverie were saints. Yet the peace and joy that radiated from both of them at their end mirrors the grace God gives to even very ordinary people when they allow him to work in their lives.

11 Love and Death

ONE OF THE GRAVEST tasks of the ministry is accompanying the dying through their last weeks, days, and hours. Death crosses every person's mind at one time or another. Yet a terminally ill person seems to face death with a more particular fear. My uncle Hans-Hermann described this fear as a dark tunnel; in the Psalms, David calls it the "valley of the shadow of death." Despite their fears, however, the dying are often very close to God, and this makes caring for them a privilege. It is as if one receives more from them than one gives. Certainly this was the case with Adela.

I had known Adela since she was a child. An outgoing young nurse, she was deeply in love with Sergei when it was discovered that she had Hodgkin's disease. Although they had made no commitment to each other, they felt sure of their love, and Adela's diagnosis only strengthened it.

Sergei told me, "I believe it is God's will for Adela and me
to be together." This touched me deeply: here was true,
God-given love – not a mere emotional or erotic attrac-
tion. Soon afterward, Adela and Sergei were engaged. I
married them in August, 1985. Never had the question of
"bearing with one another in joy and in sorrow, in health
and in sickness, until death parts you" been so real!

Humanly speaking, the new marriage didn't seem to
make sense: it began against the backdrop of a grueling
series of chemotherapy treatments, the first of which left
Adela in critical condition. For the next three years, Adela
had to undergo almost continual chemotherapy with multiple complications and frequent hospitalization. Sergei
remained loyally at her side. Then the specialists suggested a heavier course of chemotherapy combined with a
bone marrow transplant. She went through this, too, but
with no lasting benefit. Finally the couple decided to entrust everything entirely to God and to decline all further
treatment.

Throughout it all, Adela retained her sense of humor.
When she lost all her hair through chemotherapy, she
dressed up as a clown and went from ward to ward, bring-
ing joy to other patients in the hospital.

Obviously, Sergei and Adela could not hope for children
of their own, but that did not keep them from trying to
adopt a child. Nothing held them back; they were determined to tackle the bureaucratic nightmare of the adop-
tion process and to be parents. Sergei got a crib, and Adela

even prepared a layette. But nothing ever came of it. Adela died in January, 1989, after three-and-a-half years of marriage. Shortly before her passing, she wrote to her husband:

> Please, when I die remember that I was no hero, that I couldn't always accept God's will, that I was a sinner, that I failed in service and love to others, that I knew despair, depression, fear and doubt, and other temptations of the devil. Remember, too, that I loved laughter better than tears, that you can die with cancer but you can also live with it and joke about it. Please don't keep things because I made them or wrote them. They are only earthly things and nothing special. Remember rather that God's will has no "why?" – that his way is best, always; that he loves us even when we don't love him, and that in the church you never stand alone; that hope is greater than despair and faith is greater than

fear, and that God's power and kingdom one day will be victorious over everything…

Sergei has also allowed me to share a poem she wrote:

Beloved Sergei
you may find this as hard to read
as I found it hard to write
but I had to write it
even though it may be many years
before you will need it
I may outlive you
although I can't see how I could live without you
only God knows our hour
but if my time comes
God willing please be near
and tell me that it is the end
and ask me if I'm ready
to meet my maker
and hold my hand
pray for forgiveness of my sins
and pray for peace for my soul
and I'll pray for comfort for yours
and fight for you and love you
through all eternity

12 No One Knows the Hour

ARE WE READY, if death strikes unexpectedly? Can we stand before our Maker to give an account of our lives? In the Gospel of Mark (13:32–37) Jesus exhorts us to watch day and night, "for no one knows the hour of his death," only the Father. And in Matthew 25, the Parable of the Ten Virgins warns us what will happen if Jesus should return and find us indifferent and unprepared.

It is a grace when someone faced with a terminal illness is able to set things right and find peace with God before he dies, when there is time to ask forgiveness of those one may have hurt, and to find reconciliation. This grace is not granted to everyone. A person who appears healthy in the morning may be dead only a few hours later – the result of an accident or a sudden illness. Do we cherish each other? Do we realize that every encounter might be our last chance to show our love?

Hans Uli had
been a friend of mine
for years. An accom-
plished carpenter, he
was needed as a builder
when the Bruderhof
started its first Ameri-
can community, and I
traveled with him from
Paraguay to New York.
All his life he suffered
from severe asthma, and there were times when we feared
for his life. Nevertheless, he was a cheerful, outgoing person who enjoyed a good joke and loved children.

Then, one day in 1972, suddenly and completely unexpectedly, he died from a hemorrhage of the brain, leaving his wife Lizzie and eight children ranging from one
to fourteen years of age. There had been no warning signs,
nothing unusual about the way the day had begun. After
getting up early to see his eldest daughter off to high
school, he had eaten breakfast with the rest of the family.
At eight he had gone to work in our wood shop, though he
returned shortly afterwards to ask Lizzie's forgiveness for
not helping her more with the children that morning.

Toward the end of the morning someone stopped by to
exchange a few words with him. Only a short while afterwards, he was found leaning against a stack of lumber.
It was not like Hans Uli to rest at work. He explained that

he had a severe headache, and a brother helped him lie down while another ran for a stretcher. Minutes later, he was not responding. He was rushed to the hospital, but he was beyond help. He died the same evening, snatched from our midst in the prime of life. We were stunned.

In Paul's Letter to the Ephesians (4:26), he admonishes us to make peace every day before the sun goes down. Hans Uli did this, and the same day the sun went down forever on his life. It has been a comfort to his wife all these years that there was full peace and forgiveness between them before he died.

THE DEATH of Fred, another Bruderhof member who died very suddenly only a year later, was similar. Fred was an enthusiastic, hardworking brother, an engineer with a degree from Cambridge University, and he had been supervising the construction of a new dining hall at our New Meadow Run community. At ten one morning he went to see our doctor because he had chest pain. The electrocardiogram showed signs of a heart attack, and an ambulance was called. Fred's wife, Margaret, came quickly. After speaking together shortly, Margaret went to fetch what Fred would need for a hospital stay. Moments later, Fred, still lying on the examination table, said he felt dizzy. Then he became unconscious. Desperate attempts to save him were made by doctor and nurses, but they were of no avail. Advanced cardiac support was not yet developed, and defibrillators were not standard office equipment. When Margaret returned, she was met by the unbelievable news that her husband was no longer living. Within an hour her husband, our brother, was taken from us. He had had only a few seconds in which to face death.

Fred's personality was marked by strong conviction, a sense of loyalty, and a remarkable humility. A man of few words, he spoke only when he had something very important to say; otherwise he was quiet. But when he did speak, we listened.

For years, Fred had been in charge of one building crew after another, overseeing the work and keeping the supply of building materials flowing. But his greatest joy was doing the work himself. His engineering skills, highly regarded, often took him away from his family for months at a time. In the 1950s the Paraguayan government hired him to draw plans for and then supervise the building of a new hospital in Asuncion. Many years later, when one of our American communities planned a new dining hall and kitchen over a swampy field – the only available site – no engineering firm or construction company was willing to take on the project. "Bring in your English engineer," they said. So Fred designed a concrete float to support the foundation. Thirty years later, the building still stands in perfect condition.

Next to construction, there was Fred's love for the piano. It never ceased to amaze his listeners that hands so gnarled and calloused from work could play with such sensitivity and control, whether it was a Bach fugue, a Chopin etude, or an English country dance.

Now suddenly he was gone. Across the community, everything came to a halt – the wood shop closed, work on the new building stopped. Someone laid flowers at the spot where Fred had been working only hours before. What else could one do but stand in quiet reverence before such a sudden intervention of God?

THOUGH in a totally different setting, the death of five-year-old Pete was no less sudden. A happy little fellow with blond hair and blue eyes, Pete's favorite occupation was playing in the sandbox with his cars and trucks. When his kindergarten group set off on a trip to the Bronx Zoo one day in August, 1960, there was great excitement. Pete wore his new sneakers and best shirt. Little did anyone dream that it would be the last day of his life.

About three p.m. we received a call from Mt. Sinai Hospital: Pete had been admitted for what was presumed to be heat stroke. Wendell, his father, was away on business, but his mother, Pep, was immediately sent down to Manhattan. At the hospital desk she was told to her shock that her

son was on the critical list. Why? How? What had happened? She called home. Stunned, everyone rallied to see how they could help – most of all to pray for the little boy.

Despite the doctor's efforts, Pete remained comatose, and his condition worsened. An off-duty doctor came back to see if there was anything she could do; there wasn't. She sat with Pep and the others by the child's bed, silent, helpless, until about ten p.m., when the end came. No one could believe it. Just that morning he had left home so full of life! Now he was gone, and his father, though on the way home, hadn't even arrived yet.

Only the next day did the picture unfold: while the children were fascinated watching a mother monkey take care of her baby, the teachers had noticed that Pete – with them only moments before – was missing. Beside themselves with worry, they had immediately alerted zoo officials and searched every imaginable place. Finally a teacher had found him curled up, unconscious, on the back seat of the school van in the parking lot. How had he found his way among the cages, the crowds, the maze of parking lots, to the van? Only his guardian angel could have led him there. Remembering it all, Pep wrote:

> How quickly support came to us from the community at home – our own doctor to take on all the details at the hospital, and others to support me! Overwhelming thankfulness flooded over me as we came up the drive, where the love of the church welcomed me – as only those who have experienced it can know. Brothers and sisters were there waiting for me, even though it was three o'clock in the morning.

On the day after Pete's death, his classmates talked of all the things he would be seeing now – stars and galaxies, and angels. They painted a large picture of an angel carrying Pete up to heaven. Even after the wake and the burial, we could hardly believe he was gone. We felt deeply thankful for the gift of having had this little boy with us for five years, but more than that, we felt judged by how much we had taken that gift for granted. Pete's life and death reminded us of the uniqueness of each child given to us to nurture and guide. As Pep wrote further:

> God was speaking to us, and we accepted his will, even if we couldn't comprehend it then. Looking back now, thirty-six years later, I believe that a lifetime is too short to take in all that God wants to say when he calls a child to himself. Yet the important thing is to seek with all your heart, and to understand that God *is* saying something through it.

To LOSE a beloved one suddenly is always a shaking thing. Yet for an elderly person who has lived a fulfilled life, we should remember that an unexpected death can be a blessing. My father-in-law Hans, a fiery, vigorous man who thought deeply on a wide range of topics, loved nothing more than an animated discussion with anyone he met. He had been a religious socialist; later, after joining the Bruderhof, he had been imprisoned by the Nazis. Even in his old age, he was deeply interested and involved in political, social, and religious issues.

Vatter ("father") maintained an extensive correspondence with people all over the world, and even in his eighties, he traveled to visit these friends whenever he could – in Israel, Hungary, Germany, England, and his native Switzerland. Many years earlier my father had predicted, "When Hans dies, he will die in harness." And so he did.

On Christmas Eve, 1992, at the age of ninety, Vatter was sitting on a hay bale in the barn, a shepherd's cloak over his shoulders and a wooden staff in his hand, participating in our annual nativity pageant, as he had done many times before. Feeling cold, he asked to be taken home. A brother drove him back to the house, which was only a stone's throw away, then turned to help him out of the car. Vatter was gone. He had died peacefully in the back seat. On the one hand, Vatter's death came as a great shock. Yet on the other, we felt it to be a great grace. What better way to die, than peacefully, happily, on Christmas Eve?

13 Accidents

EVELYN WAS A QUIET but fun-loving thirteen-year-old who loved nature and wildlife and spent as much time as she could outdoors. A gentle, calm-natured girl, she never seemed scared or nervous, and she had a way with younger children that made them flock to her. She was a favorite babysitter among her relatives.

The summer of 1982 was unusually hot, and Evelyn was helping with the berrying and looking after the children on her uncle's farm (a Hutterite colony in Manitoba). The only relief from the heat was the river that ran along the edge of their farm. Evelyn's mother had warned her against swimming in the river – it was well known for its shifting sinkholes and sandbars – and Evelyn had promised not to go in, no matter how hot she felt.

Not one to break her word, Evelyn endured the teasing of her cousins and friends, who often waded and splashed

in the shallows. Then one day she gave in. Soon she was leading the fun with a game of water tag. One of the children spotted a sandbar a little way out and suggested that they all cross over to it. Evelyn, the tallest in the group, helped the shorter ones, and they all made it over safely.

When it was time to return home for lunch, Evelyn started back the same way, two smaller girls holding her hands. Suddenly all three heads disappeared under the water. The strong current had drawn them slightly downstream into a sinkhole. The rest of the children, still on the sandbar, shrieked in terror as they saw the three being swept downstream. An older boy heard their cries and came running, dove in, and swam to the rescue. As he reached them, all three lunged toward him, and he was overwhelmed. Knowing that unless someone let go they would all drown, he yelled, "I can't make it. Someone has to let go!" A pair of hands released their grip, and he began to make toward the shore.

Once there, he turned back for Evelyn. He knew she couldn't swim. But he could see no sign of her. By then, more help had come – divers and volunteers with boats and poles. Evelyn's parents and a crowd of relatives and neighbors gathered on the shore in shocked disbelief.

Later a farmer found her body several hundred yards downstream, caught by a tree. Amazingly, her expression reflected no terror at all. Despite the fact that she must have spent her last moments in a terrifying struggle for air, her face radiated peace and showed not one shred of fear or dread.

Though Evelyn was not a Bruderhof child, her drowning became part of our family history when my son married her sister. Almost everyone knows someone who was killed by drowning, fire, a traffic accident, a shooting, or some other traumatic form of death. Such fatalities carry with them a special burden, not only because they are unexpected, but because of their violent nature. There may be feelings of guilt and self-reproach. Often, too, there is a third party involved – someone who acted irresponsibly, someone who is to blame – in which case there is also the agonizing struggle to forgive.

IN 1958, A SLEDDING ACCIDENT at one of our English communities took the life of sixteen-year-old James. An outgoing, sports-loving young man, James certainly had his problems, like any teen, yet there remained something childlike in him. He was a child in the best sense of the word. He was always the first to greet you with a smile, to say good morning.

There was an unusual amount of snow that winter and after lunch one day, his dishwashing duty done, James

joined some friends outdoors for a rare chance to go sledding. Soon he was flying down the hill, racing his classmate Sam to the gate at the bottom of the steep hill. Then tragedy struck. James hit the gate post. At first, everyone breathed a sigh of relief – there was no obvious injury, and he had not hit his head. Soon, however, he complained of intense abdominal pain and was taken to the hospital, where he was found to be bleeding internally. The seriousness of the situation called for prayer, and the community gathered to intercede on his behalf. A few hours later James died. His last words were, "Tell Sam it wasn't his fault."

Accidents do happen. But they should never leave us untouched or unchanged. There is always a lesson to be learned: often a practical one, and always an inner one. Too many children are lost through accidents that could have been prevented, and as parents, teachers, or guardians we must continually seek to take the responsibility God has laid on us with due seriousness. Let us never be so presumptuous as to excuse a fatal accident by saying it was God's will. We ought to stop short and feel judged to the depth of our hearts, especially if it was caused by negligence.

The same applies to "close calls"; that is, accidents which almost cost a life. In such situations we should be reminded that it is only by God's grace that we are protected from day to day. A person who survives a brush with death is given a second chance at life, as it were. But at the same time it seems he has been given a warning. As my father used to say, "God is speaking a serious language" – to him and to those around him.

RARELY HAS GOD SPOKEN to us more seriously than in 1974, when tragedy ended the lives of Dwight and Jerry. Both were reliable, licensed pilots. I had flown with Dwight quite frequently. On December 30, after afternoon tea with his family, Dwight left with Jerry for a practice flight. Dwight's home, New Meadow Run, is surrounded

by high ridges, and the weather is changeable. Often, as on that fateful day, the tops of these ridges are in clouds.

When Dwight and Jerry did not return in the evening, everyone felt a heavy sense of foreboding, and brothers from our community joined the police to form a search party. Shortly after midnight the wreckage of the plane was found high on the western slope of a ridge. Jerry was still in the command pilot's seat; Dwight was lying face down, several feet from the fuselage.

The loss of these two brothers had a tremendous impact on us all. Dwight was a minister, and my father and I had worked closely together with him for many years. He and his wife Norann had twelve children, and the youngest was only seven-and-a-half weeks old. Jerry and his wife Toby were parents of five, with a sixth child on the way. Suddenly there were two widows in our midst, and seventeen fatherless children. God was surely speaking to all of us, and all of us felt challenged to open our hearts.

It was a time of mourning, to be sure, but looking back on it twenty-two years later, it also stands out as a significant time of spiritual renewal in our church. Uncannily, just days before his death, Dwight had selected a passage

for an upcoming sermon he was to give on New Year's Eve.
It began, "To be ready is everything. Let us be ready."
He did not live to see the New Year, but he was ready.

CAN A TRAGIC HAPPENING ever represent God's
will? If we claim it cannot, we are faced with a certain tension. After all, the Bible tells us it was God's will that Jesus
should suffer and die. But how can we understand and
reconcile the contradiction between the fact that God does
not want suffering and death, yet still permits them? Perhaps there is a difference between what God allows now
because of our sin – Moses called it our hardness of heart –
and his ultimate will for the future, which is his perfect
love.

George McDonald writes that sometimes tragedy strikes
like a bolt of lightning from a clear sky, and life is never the
same again. What happens then depends on our response
to the tragedy. Either we will feel driven into the arms of
God, or we will fall into despair and isolation. When we
are faced with the pain of suffering or death, let us ask
God to lead us closer to him. I am convinced that no matter what tragedy befalls us, it is his will that we should let it
lead us to a greater love for each other, and for him.

14 When Medicine Ends

I HAVE BEEN doing some thinking about my future. I just saw my doctor on Tuesday morning, and my tumor is not responding to the stronger medication I'm on. I had the big operation and then the first round of treatments, which were aimed at cure. It did not work. Now that the illness has recurred, he says any further treatment would be to prolong life, but it cannot cure the disease.

There are two options of chemotherapy, and a third option: no treatment at all. The more I think about it, the more I feel like opting for no further treatment. It is a most unpleasant experience, and everything in me balks at the idea of going through it again. Also, I can't quite face hair loss again. It is a small point but a needy one.

So I would gladly forgo further treatment and just continue to live thankfully, one day at a time. I know if I hold on to Jesus, he will walk through this valley of shadow with me. After all, he's been there himself! I truly believe the words of Job, "And though worms destroy this body, I know that my Redeemer liveth."

I will trust in God through whatever lies ahead. I know there will be very difficult times, but I want to turn more to our Heavenly Physician. He knows best how to heal. He has given me a very full life, and I'm content to give it over to him now.

Your sister Bronwen

Bronwen, forty-nine, had made up her mind. After years of battling cancer, lumps were reappearing all over her body, and she knew that nothing more could be done. Medicine had failed. Yet Bronwen did not consider her life a failure. Rather, as the letter above shows, she felt fulfilled.

When serious illness strikes, we need to try to discern as best we can what God's will might be for the stricken person. After reading Bronwen's letter, Verena and I sat together with her and her parents, her doctors, and several ministers from our church to consider her situation. Knowing that we would stand by her in the difficult days ahead, and that her family, too, would be given all the support they needed, we agreed to accept her decision to forgo further medical treatment. Bronwen's response moved us: "I have a sense of peace about what lies ahead. You do what you can for as long as you can, and in the end all that is left is prayer."

Often such an action is viewed as a premature giving-up. But there is a time to recognize that a person is indeed dying and that further medical intervention will only cause

more anguish. In their relentless pursuit of cures, physicians too often view death as a failure. Sometimes they are so intent on prolonging life that they even disregard very clear signs that a person's condition is irreversible, that treatment is futile, and death inevitable. (This does not mean that we at the Bruderhof take matters into our own hands; in every case, we provide the best medical help available, and we reject every aspect of euthanasia as a sin.)

Sometimes, especially when a person has cancer, we are confronted by the question of how far to go with medical treatment. Certainly we are not opposed to medical progress. We run professionally staffed clinics at each of our Bruderhof communities, and our doctors and nurses confer with local doctors' offices and hospitals to provide the best care we can afford. We are thankful for every new discovery that is made, for better chances of survival and faster relief from pain. It is only that one sometimes wonders how long the body should be kept alive while the soul is longing to be released. When it means weeks or months of pain, suffering, and separation in a hospital with only minimal improvement for the patient, questions arise: Are we keeping someone alive for *their* sake, or for the sake of scientific research? Are we trying to uphold a good professional record? a standard of medical ethics? Our only real concern should be to try to discern God's will for the suffering person. I don't mean this in a presumptuous way, certainly not in the sense of assuming to know God's will, but we do have a Body of believers, we have each other, and we believe that God wants to lead us. The whispers of the good Spirit can be heard by a gathered church. Let us always remain sensitive to its leading.

WHEN MY NEPHEW Ed and his wife Dorli had their first child, Stephen, he was found to have many problems – with his heart, his lungs, his throat, and more. Though his doctors arranged to have everything attended to as quickly as possible, they soon realized he was dying. It seemed that this little one was not meant for this world. The hospital staff, feeling the same, permitted one of our doctors to join the parents in the neonatal ICU, where they gently removed the life-supporting apparatus. It was too painful to watch Stephen struggle with his wires, cords, and tubes – they seemed like a leash that tied his soul as well as his body. Once freed and placed in his mother's

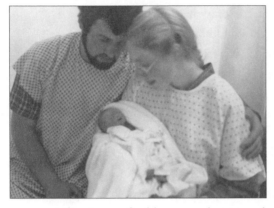

arms, Stephen's life slipped away quietly and painlessly.

Ed and Dorli sat together with the little one in their arms, trying to grasp what had just happened, and trying to find harmony between their heart's longing and God's will. Within the space of a day, God had given them new life and then taken it back to himself.

THROUGHOUT the many years we have lived together as a community, we have known countless brothers and sisters, young people, and even children who were able to find strength to face their suffering with joy, because of the love that surrounded them. There is no medicine like love. It may not bring physical healing, but often something much greater is given: healing for the soul, deepened faith, and new trust.

My father's elder brother Hardy suffered from heart disease and diabetes for many years. Hardy guided many young people to Christ during his long life, and after my father's death, when I was asked to lead the Bruderhof as its elder, Hardy was like a father to me. I often turned to him for advice.

In September, 1984, Hardy underwent cardiac bypass surgery; in November of the same year he suffered severe heart failure. Hospitalized, he asked to be released and cared for at home. In early December his blood pressure was dangerously low. At times he was restless or distressed; at other times very peaceful. During moments like these, one felt the closeness of eternity in his room. Once he said, quite simply, "You know, I am dying."

Hardy needed intravenous medications to maintain his blood pressure, and oxygen to relieve his breathing difficulties and chest pain. One day, however, he surprised everyone by trying to pull out the IV; he was just as ready to die as to live, he said – whatever God had in mind for him. We discussed the situation at length and hesitantly agreed to have the IV discontinued. The doctors believed that without the medication he could not live long, and Hardy knew this. It would be a step of faith, but we had faith. Most important, Hardy had faith.

When his nurse, one of our brothers, removed the IV, Hardy motioned him to bend over and gave him a kiss. Then, wishing to see the whole community, he asked if we could call a meeting. It was early afternoon, and people were at work, but we called everyone together. Hardy arrived in his wheelchair – no IV, no oxygen, nothing! It was shortly before Christmas. I spoke about the coming of Christ, a time of expectation for the whole world, a time of hope for those who are sick and suffering. We sang together and asked God to protect Hardy.

Miraculously, Hardy survived the next days and even improved, gaining new strength daily. Over the next weeks and months he was his old self – an active, lively member of the church. He even made several journeys, including one to Europe. Three years later, he died peacefully of heart failure. It was just as my grandmother Emmy had once written:

> With a dying person, there can sometimes be a flaring up of life just before death. There is suddenly a renewed hope for recovery – yet then he dies. It is like the coming of a bright autumn before a long, cold winter. And afterward comes spring: resurrection.

Hardy's last years showed us that there are times when medical knowledge must be put aside, and we must allow God to take over. Even today, he *does* give miracles, if only we believe in him.

15 In God's Hands

TO MANY, the Old Testament is a collection of strange,
baffling tales that have little meaning for today's world.
Yet if we have ears to hear, its stories, especially those that
describe the intervention of the divine into the human
sphere, can speak to us of God's longing to intervene in
each of our lives too.

Take the story of Daniel, for instance – here was a
prophet to Jews and Gentiles who fearlessly declared God's
purpose yet (like the other prophets) remained human.
Daniel had hopes and ambitions, fears and anxieties. What
made him unique was his love for God above all else, even
at the cost of his life. Daniel had faith that God would
never forsake him; he had the courage that conquers the
fear of death. That is why God could use him in such a
powerful way. Where are the Daniels of our day? Where

are people whose trust in God is so great that they can face death without flinching?

MERRILL was a fellow member of the Bruderhof and a minister. I worked with him for over two decades. His extensive knowledge of the Old and New Testaments brought Scripture alive for all of us; in addition he conducted choirs, counseled high school students, and served the church in many ways at several of our communities.

In the spring of 1986, Merrill developed mild symptoms that pointed to liver and pancreas troubles. Then he began to have severe nausea and vomiting. Within a few days he was diagnosed with cancer of the pancreas. Neither surgery, radiation, nor chemotherapy would be of use. He accepted the prognosis trustingly and even encouraged his wife and twelve children: "Shall I tell you something? Even before we knew this would happen, God knew it. Now we must see that through it we are brought closer together." Like Daniel before the lions, Merrill stood humanly helpless before his disease, but he continued to hold firm to God. All he had was his faith, but it was an absolute faith, a complete surrendering of all his own desires. He wrote at the time:

> My future is uncertain. The joy is knowing that it is completely in God's hands. All I have to do is thank him…If I have not much longer to live, then that is God's will and it should mean something. My task is

to find out what it means...I have no complaints, only thanks! If it is God's pleasure to give me a chance to start over again, that's wonderful. If it is not his pleasure and he has other tasks for me, I accept that. Faith doesn't depend on me having my way; faith depends on God having his way. This must be my highest joy and delight. Otherwise how can I pray, "Thy will be done"?

Friends sent him materials describing a homeopathic therapy course available in Mexico, but Merrill's answer showed that his priorities were quite different:

About the question of what to do, I have only consulted with my wife Kathy and my immediate family. Without doubting the truth or the efficacy of the method, I have nonetheless decided not to pursue this method or even to contact the institute. The reason is as follows:

Our life in the Bruderhof is a full one, and its focus is on Jesus alone, i.e., on lifelong repentance and on seeking to follow his will. To put it crassly, I would rather live, say, only another six or eight months than embark on a regimen that may or may not prolong my life but is so totally self-centered and self-saving.

My decision may seem mad to you, but I am unalterably firm in it. I joyfully place myself on the mercy of God, and I will praise him for carrying out his will on my body, even if it means physical death. I see this as a major part of my task and witness at this time.

Merrill lived exactly one more year. Unlike many others who know their time on earth is limited, he never spoke of his death; he did not want to give it even that much credit. He did not outwardly prepare for death in any way. And both within our Bruderhof communities and further afield, he continued reaching out to others. He spent more time, not less, with his children and grandchildren, and with young adult groups – he counseled, sang, even rehearsed and directed a musical with them. Despite increasing pain and discomforts, he traveled to all our communities, holding meetings and performing baptisms and marriages, often to the point of exhaustion.

Because Merrill felt it a privilege to suffer, he was able to meet the most difficult moments in good humor. He would even do things that were medically unreasonable, in order to show his defiance of his illness. Unforgettable for us all was the evening he conducted Mendelssohn's *Elijah* shortly before he died, putting his whole soul and body into the music and even singing several solo numbers.

A few months before his death, Merrill wrote to a friend in Germany who was also dying of cancer:

> I feel very close to you because I also have a condition that the doctors see very little hope for. I'm in the best possible hands – God's hands – a situation I actually rejoice in. I could not be better off.
>
> In fact, you and I know that sickness came into the world only because of sin. This burdens and grieves God beyond our understanding. Jesus suffered because of it. Now you and I are privileged to suffer with him… May God grant that we always see it so, and glorify him alone. And if he should choose to give our earthly lives back to us for a longer time, may we use them only to do his wonderful will. Either way, we love and thank and praise him.

Merrill's dying was not unusual in itself; what *was* remarkable was the inner vigor with which he faced his last months. He accepted his illness as being allowed by God, but he did not believe it had been sent by him. He went down fighting, not for his own salvation but for the glory of God. His death came as a great loss to our whole church and to me personally.

To ALL appearances a healthy baby, Matthew Ray (born 1967) became jaundiced when he was two weeks old. Soon it was discovered that he had no bile ducts connecting his liver and intestines – a rare condition that can sometimes be corrected today but was virtually untreatable at the time. An operation at Yale confirmed the serious nature of the problem: the surgeon said that Matthew would not live for more than fourteen months. His parents, Peter and Susanna, were devastated as they took their baby: he was going home to the family, home to the church, but he was also going home to die.

Until he was six months old, Matthew developed normally, though he was always a little yellow. Then he began to go downhill. First he stopped gaining, and then he began to lose weight. His stomach became distended, his face pinched. As his father later said, he looked like a starving child – skin and bone, and big, wide eyes. Thankfully, his older brothers and sister never noticed those things. They never even took in the fact that he was sick; they just loved him as he was.

Just as the doctor had predicted, Matthew died when he was fourteen months old. At the end his skin was a dark orange, and he weighed only eight pounds.

Even today, no medical knowledge can guarantee that a dying child will live. But if he dies we can be assured that he has gone to God, and his death should draw us close to God too. At Matthew's funeral service my father said: "When you look into the eyes of children, you can see something of heaven." A similar thought is expressed below in a poem written for Peter and Susanna after Matthew's death by Jane Clement, a friend and fellow member of the community:

> Little child – God holds you in His hand.
> In your deep eyes, which we have seen with pain,
> we glimpsed the promise of that hidden land,
> the hope of victory, of the coming reign.
>
> Now at the Master's side your feet will run
> across the fields of Heaven, and your hands
> will gather angel flowers, the buttercups
> of starry meadows far beyond our sight,
> and you will grow and blossom in the light.
>
> For He who was a Child and bore our sin
> has opened wide the gate to take you in.

16 Suffering

WHENEVER I think of suffering, Miriam comes to mind. Born with multiple physical handicaps, including the inability to swallow, she had to be fed by dropper for the first few weeks of her life and by feeding tube until she was one year old. But it was "brittle bone disease" that affected her most severely. As a toddler she would sometimes break a bone just by trying to pull her leg out from between the bars of her crib. Later, tripping over a rug or bumping into a doorframe could mean a series of fractures in her arms or legs or both, often followed by hospitalization and surgery, and always accompanied by much pain, as well as six weeks or more in a cast. By age eight, Miriam had broken her legs sixteen times. In her short life of twenty-eight years, she was hospitalized more than forty times, had hundreds of fractures, and underwent at least fifteen operations.

Though Miriam's bones were weak, her character
was indomitable. Hopping around on her little crutches,
weighed down by heavy metal leg braces, she reminded
more than one person of a sparrow: small, spunky,
cheerful.

Slowly, Miriam's dependence on crutches caused the
bones in her arms to bend so badly that the doctors had to
forbid her to use them, and she was restricted to a wheelchair. She still was fully part of her class, and ways were
found to include her in every activity possible. With a
lightweight chair set on bicycle wheels, or a chair on long
poles carried by the boys in her class, she could even join
hikes on mountain trails. Later she rejoiced when she was
given a new electric wheelchair. Now she could go wher-
ever she pleased! No one who knew her will be able to
forget the way she buzzed around our community, stop-
ping to talk to everyone she met.

Miriam was a creative person, always busy drawing,
painting, writing, or sewing, even with her crippled hands.
An avid reader, she wrote poetry and did well in school.
Because of her many frailties, she had to be taught at
home, but at the end of the twelfth grade she participated
in the graduation ceremonies at the local high school. After
handing her her diploma, the principal bent over to kiss
her, and the audience applauded thunderously.

Even as an adult, Miriam was a very small person –
only four feet tall and eighty pounds. Her crooked spine
reduced her lung volume and affected her heart. She was
always short of breath and suffered heart failure already

at ten. During a hospitalization in 1979, the specialists expected her to live only one more year; at one point they gave her only ten more days. Little did anyone guess that she would live another twelve years.

Miriam's suffering was not limited to her physical condition. When she was fourteen, her mother died unexpectedly – a tremendous shock to Miriam. Despite the hard times that followed, Miriam refused to let her difficulties get her down. My father wrote to her at the time, "The church will now be your mother, and you will be a child of the church" – and she gratefully accepted this.

Another time he wrote to her, "There are many people who have a strong body and a dull soul. You have a weak body, but a living soul. Thank God for this."

When I baptized Miriam in 1983, she believed, in her childlike way, that she might experience healing. She longed to walk and run like everyone else. Instead, God gave her another gift: in her utter dependence on him, he used her to touch the lives of others.

Miriam's last month was an intense struggle for life and breath. Her little body did not let go of life easily, and she suffered greatly. But she was not afraid of death.

She had sensed for years that her life would not be long, and she had a childlike view of Paradise. When nothing more could be done medically, she said, through her oxygen mask, "Well, I think I'm ready. I only have a few more thank-you notes to write."

Through Miriam's life it is possible to glimpse at least part of what Paul must have meant in Romans 8:17 when he wrote, "We share in his suffering so that we may share in his glory." These words were often on my father's mind when there was sickness or a death in our church. In connection with this passage, he once said, "The experience of suffering should always bring us very close together, for when one member suffers, then the whole church suffers, and all feel the pain and carry it in faith."

DEB, ANOTHER sister in our community, grew up near Boston in a wealthy family. As a child, she had toured Europe with her parents, taken summer vacations on Martha's Vineyard, and been educated in private schools.

In 1950, after graduation from Smith College, Deb married, and soon she and her husband Charles settled down in a cooperative community in California. Continued seeking for a deeper purpose in life led them to our Bruderhof, where they decided to join us for good.

When Deb was forty-three, she began to experience numbness in her hands and feet. No medical explanation could be found. Not one to complain, she quietly bore the bothersome problem as it slowly worsened, even though she was raising a family of six. The weakness grew worse. One of her children's playmates still remembers his surprise when Tommy told him, "Mama can't buckle my boots anymore or help me with my zipper." Family walks became shorter, and Deb began to be unsteady. She had to use both hands to lift a carton of milk. Still, she bravely insisted on continuing to fulfill her motherly tasks.

Early in 1969, however, a tumor was found in the back of her neck, and she was hospitalized. An emergency operation removed the tumor, but the surgery left her totally paralyzed below the neck. Almost completely helpless, she could communicate only with her eyes. Her life had been spared, but her body was in ruins.

Deb was determined to become fully functional again. Several times a week she saw her physical therapist, and every day she strained to re-teach her muscles to do what she wanted them to do. Part of it was her personality – she had always been a fighter – but there was also another incentive for regaining strength as quickly as possible: she was expecting a child. Six months after her operation, Deb gave birth to a boy. Miraculously, Mark was strong and healthy in every way, even after all his mother had been through in the previous months. Mark's arrival brought great delight to the family; he was not an added burden but a source of new joy and inner strength. Charles and Deb felt God's love through this gift: "His ways are past our understanding."

Deb was not able to care for her baby, but she did all she could. She was too weak to hold him for any length of time, yet propped up with pillows, she still managed to give him his bottle.

When Mark was six weeks old, Deb entered a rehabilitation program to relearn the daily activities and skills she had taken for granted all her life, but could no longer perform: walking, writing, tying her shoes, buttoning her blouse, combing her hair, cracking an egg. Despite the tremendous efforts she made, her recovery was only partial: walking remained difficult, her writing was poor, and she was still weak.

Over the next years she courageously battled her physical hindrances with cheerfulness and humor. She still had her large family around her, of course, and she insisted on caring for them as much as she could. Then, almost imperceptibly, she began to lose what little strength she had. A second operation, and then a third, did not help. For the last five years of her life she was confined to a reclining wheelchair; her body was too weak to support even the weight of her own head and arms.

Even then, however, she refused to give up. Debilitated as she was physically, she remained mentally and spiritually alert. Until a week before her death, she put in several hours a day proofreading for our publishing house with another sister.

Deb did not have cancer, multiple sclerosis, or any of the many other disabling diseases of our time. She had only a small growth, in itself harmless enough, that appeared in the wrong place. It changed the course of her life.

Deb's whole attitude to her suffering is summed up in her reply to a well-meaning visitor who told her: "If you ask Jesus, he can make you well again." "I know," Deb said. "But he has given me something much more wonderful – a life together with brothers and sisters." At her memorial service, her neurosurgeon said that of all his thousands of patients, he felt most privileged to care for Deb – he always felt as if he was ministering to Christ, because Christ lived in her so visibly. This is the challenge that we are left with: to become Christ-like in adversity, in suffering. It will never be easy, but as we are promised, we will be sent "the Comforter, the Holy Spirit" (Jn. 15:26), who brings us inner strength and deep peace of heart.

17 Faith

ED WAS ONE of a kind – a single man with a southern drawl and a big heart. Formerly an executive for a large Georgia trucking company, he joined our community when he was already in his fifties. The first time he visited, he said he felt he had found the pearl of great price. Unpretentious and spontaneous, he had the faith of a child: it was based, very simply, on a firm belief in the goodness and mercy of God.

Yet he was far from pious. Ed always said exactly what he thought, giving a running commentary on life – sometimes humorous, sometimes serious, sometimes appropriate, sometimes not. Ed never married and had no family, yet he loved people, and his room was always full of teenagers shooting the breeze and listening to "Achy, breaky heart" or others of his country-western favorites. Ed was a teacher as much as a friend and brother, yet he was never

moralistic: he provided stability, friendship, and fun at the same time. Late one evening, when three boys were singing loudly below his window, he poked his head out and called them to come in: "Sing for me inside – that's the most beautiful singing I've ever heard!"

Always unassuming, Ed often signed notes or letters he wrote with "Edwin Glover Buxton, L.B." ("lowly brother"). He never missed an opportunity to express his thanks. When he had to call his nurse for pain medication, he would give him a bone-breaking handshake or a big hug, look into his eyes, and say emphatically, "My dear lowly brother-man, are you listening? Thanks a million!"

Ed suffered from heart disease all the years he was with us and he was fully aware that he could die at any time. Sometimes he spoke about his faith and about death. Once he told my son, who was one of his nurses, that he was looking forward to meeting God: "I mean, it will be awesome and fearsome, but God and I know each other. He knows about my sinful past. And, you know, he also knows I'm sorry for it." Certainly Ed did not want his death to be a "big deal." In fact, he even instructed his teenage friends to carry his casket down a shortcut through the woods to the cemetery and "maybe bump into a few trees."

Ed knew that faith and a good conscience go hand in hand; he knew the power of confession and believed in forgiveness. One day he asked me to come to his room, where he shared several things that were on his conscience – nothing very significant, but things that burdened him. Then he asked me, "Am I forgiven?" I assured him: "Ed, you know that Jesus gave the Church the authority to forgive sins. In the name of Jesus, yes, you are forgiven." He embraced me and said that this was one of the most wonderful moments of his life. "Now I can meet eternity with great joy." Fully assured of his peace with God, he died in his bed at five a.m. a few days later. In his pocket we found this note:

> Around 7:30 or 7:40 p.m. I was sitting here, about to have supper, and I felt a tremendous sorrow for having offended God and sinned against him, a feeling greater than I have ever had before. It could be that I am approaching eternity, and I wanted my people here to know about it. Ed.

Ed's death left none of us untouched, and it marked a turning point in the lives of many of the young men he had befriended. Greg, fifteen, wrote this poem at the time:

> I feel empty inside,
> As though something was gone.

Hollowness, nothingness
Fills the spot where you were.

It's like you were lost
And I had no way to find you.
Although it seems you're lost to me
I know you're home (or on your way)!

ANOTHER PERSON whose dying had an impact on
our communities, though under completely different circumstances, was my uncle Hans-Hermann. A tall, gaunt
man, he had been a farmer, a teacher, and a minister treasured for his inner sensitivity and discernment; now, after
decades of smoking, he had developed severe emphysema.

In August, 1972, Hans-Herman was diagnosed with
lung cancer. I was sitting with my father when he and his
wife Gertrud called us with the news. It was a great shock.
Papa had always been close to his younger brother, and
Hans-Hermann was only fifty-seven years old. His condition was already far advanced, and the doctors told us
that we could expect little help, either from surgery or
radiation.

During the months that remained, Hans-Hermann
suffered greatly from "air hunger" and needed oxygen at
all times. Spiritually he was very lively. One morning when
I visited him, he was deep in thought and said, "It's hard

to be suspended between life and death like this. We are very much attached to life; that must have a deep significance. I believe that one day, from the other side of eternity, we'll be able to understand it better." Another time he said: "Our sins prevent us from looking into eternity. Sometimes it is like a thin veil, other times like a heavy curtain. It all depends on our nearness to God."

Hans-Hermann's acceptance of his suffering moved many in our church, and the spiritual renewal he found through his illness spread among our communities. In reminding us of the essentials of discipleship, he also helped many to face their inner deadness and inspired them to seek their first love anew.

Hans-Hermann lived until December. Again and again we prayed for his recovery; as we read in James 5, "the prayer of faith will save the sick man." Yet we had to acknowledge that the gift of healing was simply not given to us as it was to the first disciples.

A week or so before Christmas, on a Sunday morning, he woke early, and we decided to bathe him. Just as we were finishing, Gertrud came in. We told her that everything was done, except that we had left his hair for her to comb. Suddenly, Hans-Hermann removed his oxygen mask and smiled, a radiant look of joy and peace spreading over his face. Sensing that the end was near, we called the rest of the family. Stretching out both arms to Gertrud, he clasped her hands. They looked at each other – a last, long look – and then he was gone. My father said later, "In his face we saw something victorious. I cannot express it otherwise than to say that it was the joy of accepting God's will and God's hour." Neither Milton (Hans-Hermann's doctor), nor Papa, nor I had ever seen anyone face the last moment so consciously and joyously.

Since Hans-Hermann's death, I have been at the bedside of many dying people, and I have seen over and over again that, ultimately, this faith – which means acceptance of God's will – is all that matters. Without it, death is a terrifying nightmare; with it, one is mysteriously armed to meet the last moments willingly, and with joy.

18 Prayer and Healing

IT WAS EARLY SUMMER, 1935, and Edith lay dying in a wooden hut at the Alm, our community high in the Liechtenstein Alps. She was only twenty-four, but already it appeared as though her life were at an end. A few days earlier she had given birth to her first child. Now she had developed childbed fever (universally fatal in that day and age) and the infection had spread to her bloodstream. Her temperature was high, her pulse had quickened, her veins were inflamed, her body swollen. Edith was dying, and there seemed to be no hope of recovery.

Edith was my aunt. Drawn to our community after meeting my uncle Hardy at Tübingen University, she wanted to join it; when her parents found out, however, her father locked her in a second-story bedroom. It was only by escaping in the middle of the night, with the aid of a bed sheet twisted into a rope, that she was able to

follow the call she felt. Once at the Bruderhof, she soon became a dedicated member.

Now, only two years later, she seemed doomed to die. Still, the little group of brothers and sisters who had gathered around her asked God for her life to be spared if it were his will. Following the Letter of James (5: 14–15), my grandfather Eberhard laid his hands on her – knowing he himself could do nothing, but believing, as did Edith, that God can overcome all things, even "sickness unto death."

The knowledge that the church was standing with her in faith gave Edith remarkable strength, and for a time it even looked as though there might be a turning point. Yet there were also hours when it seemed she might be taken at any minute. All the same, the circle of brothers and sisters around Edith persisted in prayer, and my grandfather repeated the laying on of hands in the name of Christ each evening for several days. Again and again it seemed she found new energies: moreover, she felt that the powers of death were being driven out by God's power at work in her body. Certain that it was God's will that she should live –

not for her own sake or even for the sake of her child or her husband, but as a witness to his power in the church – she exclaimed: "My life is beginning again, quite new!" Eventually, Edith recovered from her illness completely.

IN PRAYING for healing (or, for that matter, anything else) we must seek the will of God. But we must also simply *believe.* Certainly we must remain open to God's plan for each person – it may not include physical healing – yet why shouldn't we believe fully that God *can* give what we ask of him?

We have seen the power of prayer over sickness and death many times in the history of our church. One of the more unforgettable incidents was the case of my father's cousin Hermann, a former member of the Hitler Youth who experienced conversion, denounced Nazism, and joined the Bruderhof at twenty years of age. As a young man, Hermann had severe tuberculosis of the lungs; in his fifties, during a relapse, he was diagnosed with lung cancer. During surgery a tumor the size of a baseball was removed (as well as part of one lung), and the doctors predicted he would not live more than a year or two. Radiation and chemotherapy, they said, would be of no benefit.

Then, at a time when the outlook could not have been grimmer, our church began to pray actively for Hermann's life. Before long, he grew strong and even healthy again. Recovering fully, he lived for eighteen more years and traveled repeatedly between the United States and Europe, mostly on behalf of our publishing house. He died only when pneumonia took him in 1990 at the age of seventy-four.

WHEN SIMON arrived in February of 1996, I was as thrilled as his parents were. I had known Simon's father and mother since they were children, and I had counseled them during the time of their engagement and married them. Now, after three years of waiting and praying for a child, they finally had one – a little boy. He was a beautiful, healthy, six-pound baby, perfect in every way.

Six hours later, he developed difficulty breathing. Oxygen was brought immediately, and an ambulance took him to the hospital. On the way, Simon turned blue; he began to grunt with every breath, nostrils flaring. Then a chest X-ray showed severe infection in both lungs. Clearly, the child was in critical condition. If he survived, his parents were told, he would sustain hearing loss, visual impairment, perhaps even brain damage.

Heavy-hearted with the the awful news, we struggled to shut out the doctors' words, turning instead in prayer to God. Why shouldn't we? God knew things the doctors didn't. Beneath the maze of wires, needles, tubes, and lights, beneath the hum of the mechanical ventilator breathing for him, wasn't Simon himself also fighting for life?

By evening the baby grew worse: he was bleeding from his lungs and needed a transfusion. Then his blood pressure dropped. Dopamine, a powerful drug, was started, but Simon's life was hanging in the balance. Back at home, however, another force was being enlisted to fight for Simon – something far more powerful than dopamine: the common prayer of dozens of brothers and sisters who, woken up by telephone calls from house to house, had gathered to pray, just as Simon's parents and those supporting them prayed at the hospital. The little boy fought bravely on.

At midnight it happened: Simon turned the corner. By five a.m. the oxygen was turned down. The doctor, who had not left the baby all night, looked up and said, "My God, you people know how to pray! I can't explain otherwise why he is still here." Another doctor was more blunt. "Your child should have died," she said, shaking her head in disbelief.

Not only did Simon pull through that long and dreadful

night, but he steadily improved over the next days without a single setback, despite the doctors' prediction of many ups and downs on the road to recovery. Before long Simon was discharged. Now, months later, Simon is a healthy, chubby little boy, and there is no neurological damage of any kind.

Edith and Hermann's lives were given back to them through prayer. Simon's life, too, is a testimony to its power: "Ask and it will be given to you; seek and you will find; knock and the door will be opened to you. For everyone who asks receives; he who seeks finds; and to him who knocks, the door will be opened" (Mt. 7:7–8). All three lives are also a testimony to the importance of faith. Jesus said that if we have faith as small as a mustard seed, mountains can be moved. Even mountains of illness, even shadows of death.

19 Caring

ONLY TWO or three generations ago, many people lived out their lives in one place. They raised their children, grew old, and died in their homes, surrounded by family and friends and church. In most sectors of society today – marked as it is by mobility and rootlessness – the sense of belonging to a particular community has been lost. Nowadays, for whatever reason, aging parents often lose what few close connections they have with their children by midlife and enter old age in loneliness. For the most part they are cared for not by their own loved ones, but by people who are hired to do it. Sometimes they are moved from one nursing home to another, with new people and new surroundings causing confusion and depression.

My heart goes out to the many thousands of elderly people hidden away in nursing homes, separated from those they love, waiting to die. Perhaps this is a necessary evil of our time. I am well aware of the difficulties encountered in arranging the practical aspects of care for the elderly, especially in the family home. But we need to cherish one another more, and see that our words of love are matched by our deeds; that is the "hands and feet" of the gospel. Mother Teresa writes:

> I can never forget a visit I made to a nursing home where they kept all these old parents of sons and daughters who had put them into the institution and forgotten them. In this home these old people had everything – good food, comfortable places, television, everything. But they were not smiling, and nearly everyone was looking toward the door. And Sister said, "This is the way it is nearly every day. They are expecting, they are hoping, that a son or daughter will come to visit them. They are hurt because they are forgotten."[7]

Even in cases where people do not forget their aging parents, they often have very little love for them. A young woman at our community who used to work in a nursing home tells me that it is not unusual for families of a dying parent to regard their last hours as nothing more than an inconvenience. When calling a dying man's children on behalf of the nursing home, for instance, she was told, "Call us when he's gone, but don't bother us if it's during the night." Did it never cross their minds that their father needed them *before* he died?

In the face of such callousness it is not surprising that the elderly often feel abandoned and useless to the point where many contemplate suicide, and plenty do take their own lives. This is especially sad because they have so much to give, despite all the care they need.

AT EIGHTY-NINE, Karl needed continuous care. Born in Germany at the beginning of the century, he had been abused as a child; eventually he ran away from home. Then he had become active in the labor movement. Imprisoned in 1936 for his outspoken opposition to National Socialism, he had escaped over the border to Holland, emigrated to England, then to Paraguay, and finally to the United States.

Karl must have read every book in the library, many two or three times, and he had kept up with contemporary issues and events with a passion unmatched by most people his age. Now he couldn't even get dressed by himself, or lift his spoon, or comb his hair.

Karl was a rebel against old age, and it didn't make his care any easier. He could get upset with you when you didn't let him walk alone (it wasn't safe), or when he couldn't hear what you were saying (he was nearly deaf). All the same, everybody loved him. Children stopped their play when he went by in his wheelchair. They ran to him, showing him dandelions, telling him secrets. *"Ja, Ja,"* he would say happily, not understanding a word. Teenagers loved him. Despite his age he was "with it": he read the papers, knew what was going on, and was keenly interested in anything they could tell him about school, youth group activities, the books they were reading, and so on. When Karl visited our woodworking shop, one brother after another would stop his work to greet him. Each one had something to talk about. And Karl, for his part, gave them his full attention.

Karl had mastered the art of being a brother. He knew how to love, but he never took the love that he received in return for granted. Before going to bed he often said, "I am sorry I was angry. Forgive me."

Even in old age, Karl refused to stop working. His job – transcribing old German manuscripts from our archives into Roman letters – was hardly easy. His hands were so shaky and his eyesight so poor that sometimes it took him an hour to transcribe one paragraph. But no one could have stopped him. His heart was filled with purpose, his eyes on the future: "These words must not be lost! They are so important!"

Karl had the good fortune that all old people deserve. He was loved. He was cared for. He was surrounded by a community. Most important, he was a part of that community, a member with something to contribute.

NO MATTER how frail, incapacitated, or disoriented an elderly person becomes, we must never forget that he or

she still has something to give. Even a demented person can bring something to us, if only our hearts are open to receive it.

As a schoolboy, I knew Bernard well and liked to work with him in our horse stables. He seemed strong as an ox, reason enough to make him one of my boyhood heroes. A generation later, as a seventy-five-year-old grandfather, he was faced with a slow loss of all his skills and faculties through Alzheimer's disease. Bernard was a gifted man with a wide variety of interests (among other things, he was an avid rose gardener) and a hard worker. Now – though one only had to read his eyes to feel his pain – he could not even communicate his most basic needs.

As Bernard's illness progressed, he could no longer

recognize his own family, not even Eileen, his wife of nearly fifty years. All the same, his personable warmth remained, and it continued to evoke love and compassion from those around him.

I have noticed this not only with Bernard, but with many others: again and again, the terminally (and chronically) ill bring to those of us who are well a profound experience of God. In this way they do us an inner service that is perhaps even more valuable than the achievements and contributions they made earlier, while still capable and strong.

Bernard saved his last smile for a baby brought to visit him. He loved little children, and they loved him. To them, he was simply another grandfather, someone to be treasured and loved – not a disoriented, dying man. That should be our attitude too: that every human life has infinite worth.

In recent decades, society's fundamental approach to life has become severely warped by selfishness. How often do we judge others (even if subconsciously) by their usefulness to us, or by how much they interfere with our careers or our pleasures? How many of us, if we are entirely honest with ourselves, have at one time or another seen the mentally retarded, the physically disabled, or the elderly as a nuisance or a strain on our time and energy?

Increasingly, close relatives, even spouses, are tempted to avoid the burden of caring for family members with chronic conditions. No one would deny that it *is* a burden.

One must also acknowledge that there are plenty of families who would be more than happy to care for their loved ones if circumstances allowed it. For them, their inability to care for their own parents is agonizing and even unbearable. Yet the most burdensome task can become a privilege to perform when approached with an attitude of love.

Unfortunately, love and respect for the elderly, the chronically ill, and the disabled are no longer priorities in our culture. More and more, euthanasia and physician-assisted suicides are losing their shock value; no longer taboo, they are now seen in many quarters as rational options. Jack Kevorkian, America's famed "Dr. Death," has assisted over forty suicides in recent months, yet in most media coverage of him there is no hint of outcry – only disinterested reportage. In Europe it is the same. An article a friend recently sent me from England quotes a doctor who excused himself from charges of physician-assisted suicide by claiming, "It could have taken another week before she died, and I needed the bed."[8]

Often the hardness of heart that accompanies the justification of these evils is masked by distorted language: people speak of "mercy killing," of "helping" the elderly die "with dignity." But even these euphemisms cannot hide the cold utilitarianism that underpins such attitudes toward the suffering of others. How tragic when people feel that the only way they can solve another's need is to help him or her die! The terminally ill need love and comfort, not death by overdose or carbon monoxide.

My MOTHER-IN-LAW Margrit suffered for thirteen years from Lou Gehrig's disease, and for the last eight years of her life she was bedridden. Margrit (we called

her *Muetti,* Swiss for "mother") was blessed with a large family: she and her husband Hans had eleven children, more than sixty grand-children, and many great-grandchildren. In her youth Muetti, a graduate of the Zurich Conservatory, had been a gifted violinist. She directed our community choir for years, and countless children learned to play and love the violin under her tutelage.

Muetti was a quiet, unassuming woman. When I think of her, I am reminded of the words "still waters run deep." There was a quietness about her that spoke louder than words. Once, at an engagement celebration, she was asked whether there was anything she might like to say to the new couple. Muetti took out her violin and played a piece instead, in this way sharing her deepest feelings of the mo-ment. Another time years later, during an animated discus-sion with guests visiting our community, Hans suddenly turned to her and asked, "What do you think, Muetti?" She smiled and said, "I listen."

Toward the end of her life Muetti was entirely incapacitated and depended on her family for everything. Still, she
accepted her condition with great patience and yielded-
ness. Speech came only with effort. At the end, she could
speak only in whispers. She could no longer do anything
for herself, "but," she whispered falteringly, "I can pray."
Muetti knew that love surrounded her, and this love – like
her own, which radiated to those who nursed her day and
night – kept her alive.

The life of every person has an infinite potential to
honor God. Isn't that why we exist? If we who call ourselves Christians are true to our calling, we will encourage
that potential, that flame, to the very end, not snuff it out
simply because it has begun to falter. Ultimately, our compassion for those who are unable to take care of themselves
is meaningless unless it translates into willing action – into
deeds of tenderness and love. If God is to be honored
through our love to others, we must be brothers and sisters
to them. We *are* our brother's keeper.

20 Dying

DYING IS THE INEVITABLE, final stage of life as we know it on earth, and only the person who is taken suddenly and unexpectedly is spared its accompanying struggle. Instinctively, each one of us resists dying with every fiber of his or her being, and it must be so, for death is life's most powerful enemy. The tenacious will to live, together with a firm belief in God, can overcome unbelievable odds. But even though a person may pull through an episode of illness, eventually physical life comes to an end.

Without question, the advanced medical technology available to us today saves and extends life. But it has also become increasingly clear in recent decades that it often prolongs dying. For the patient, this can be both a blessing and a curse. Relief of pain is of paramount importance for the dying person – oxygen, for instance, will relieve the pain of air hunger – yet the tangle of intravenous lines and wires and the beeping of electronic monitors can be so disturbing as to rob the patient of any real measure of peace. It is simply a fact that in the home there is a familiarity, warmth, and comfort – and above all else, a haven of love – that even the best hospital cannot provide.

I am well aware that most families cannot provide the constant care and nursing that a terminally ill person requires, even with the growing number of home health-care agencies that can be turned to for assistance. There are also hospices for the dying. Both in Europe and America, the hospice movement has done much in the last decades not only for the dying, but also for their families.

The hospice movement developed as a direct response to the often overly-prolonged treatment of terminal patients, the unsatisfactory level of pain control, and the increasing lack of peacefulness around so many hospital beds. A hospital is a good place to be for surgery, but as studies have shown in case after case, it is better, in the long run, for a terminally ill patient to receive support at home, in the loving care of family members and friends. They are, after all, the ones who have accompanied him thus far through life; why shouldn't they be the ones to surround him at the holy moment of crossing over into the next world?

A dying person has few needs, and fewer wants. One of the most important is his need to feel that, despite his utter dependence on the help of others, he is still respected as a person. Things as simple as wiping the lips, smoothing a wrinkled sheet, fluffing a pillow, repositioning him, or sponging his face with cool water do more than make a person comfortable: they tell him you care.

It is important to keep in mind that even after a dying person has become unresponsive, he may still hear what is being said about him. Talk to him, sing to him, encourage him, and pray with him.

As a dying person loses ground, it is essential to support him in his relationship with God. In reminding him of God's mercy and the promise of eternal life, in reading him an encouraging verse from the Bible, or singing (or playing) a favorite song, an anxious person will find new strength. This does not necessarily need many words, of course: one can also simply hold his hand and sit silently with him.

It is vital that there be an atmosphere of peace around the bedside of a dying person. This is no time to bring up old grievances, family quarrels, and unresolved issues from the past, unless settling these by means of an apology or reassurance will bring reconciliation. Most crucial, the dying must never be made to feel emotionally or spiritually isolated in any way. Their suffering must be *our* suffering – they cannot be left to feel that they are going through their last hours on their own.

Dying involves one's whole being – one's body, one's emotions, one's spirit. Indeed, it involves not only the departing person himself, but those around him, who experience a tangle of emotions: dread, anguish, sorrow, hope, exhaustion, and pain. You may be anxious, uncomfortable, distraught: that is quite natural. Yet no matter how heavy or depressed you feel, help the dying person and yourself to find inner peace, and remind him that looking forward to eternity can and should be a joyful thing.

Dorothy Day brings this thought to expression in a wonderful way, and not only in the context of helping a dying person face death, but in the broader sense of questioning our conventional attitude to eternity:

> We may be living on the edge of eternity, but that should not make us dismal. The early Christians rejoiced to think that the end of the world was near, as they thought. Are we so unready to face God? Are we so avid for joys here, that we perceive so darkly those to come?[9]

SOMETIMES THE DYING may experience glimpses of eternity that can draw the whole circle around their bed into an atmosphere of closeness to God and love to each other – times when the Spirit reaches out to us through the dying person. Live for these moments. Live for love and peace.

Dying may take a long time. For the caregivers as well as for the patient, there will be endless hours, long days and longer nights. All the same, the final moment may come quickly and unexpectedly, and family members should never take their presence at the moment of departure for granted. A few years ago a grandfather in one of our communities passed away. For more than a week, all of his children had been at his side day and night. When the end came early one morning, however, most of them were not present. Emotionally devastated, they reproached themselves for having failed their father in his last hours. On the one hand I could understand their feelings of guilt; on the other, I felt I needed to remind them that no one is ever alone at the moment of death. God's angels are always around the dying, and they will lead them as they leave this earth.

It is painful to witness the physical changes – the emaciation, the distortion of features – that occur in the face of a beloved one on the threshold of death. At the moment of departing, however, another change may be visible, prefiguring the resurrection and the life beyond. We may see a smile, a new look in the eyes, perhaps an unexpected movement or speech, as if the dying one is standing on the edge of eternity. At moments like these, we see more clearly than ever the unique beauty of each soul as it shines through, giving us a hint of a new, gloriously healed body:

> What is sown is perishable, what is raised is imperishable. It is sown in dishonor, it is raised in glory. It is sown in weakness, it is raised in power. It is sown a physical body, it is raised a spiritual body (1 Cor. 15:42–44).

We have experienced again and again the blessings of gathering in a spirit of love around a person at the hour of his death, at a time when the only relationship that matters is that between the dying person and God. We cannot look into his heart, nor can we judge how he stands before God, but we can pray that his soul is given grace. And we can trust that he is in God's hands.

21 Grieving

WHEN YOU LOSE a beloved one, the deep grief
that follows continues for a long time. It is hard to imagine
that life will ever be right or normal again. Grief is a completely natural and healthy response to a death, and it
should not be repressed. It is the soul's expression of continuing love for that person and the way to its healing. Too
often, families and friends do not permit themselves to
mourn their loss: they try to "get over it," to shut it out
of their mental foreground, or to move on to other things.
And often, without even realizing it, they harden their
hearts against God in the process.

Not long after my mother died, our family was sitting
around the table together with my father, drinking coffee.
We were all adults – married, with our own families – and
we were chatting about our children, laughing, and trading
jokes. This hurt my father. He admonished us for letting

life get back to normal so quickly, and for failing to take Mama's death more seriously. Couldn't we see he was still grieving deeply? Shouldn't we be grieving too? I have never forgotten Papa's challenge.

Anne Morrow Lindbergh writes:

> One must grieve, and one must go through periods of numbness that are harder to bear than grief. One must refuse the easy escapes offered by habit and human tradition. The first and most common offerings of family and friends are always distractions ("Take her out" – "Get her away" – "Change the scene" – "Bring in people to cheer her up" – "Don't let her sit and mourn," when it is mourning one needs)...
>
> Courage is a first step, but simply to bear the blow bravely is not enough. Stoicism is courageous, but it is only a halfway house on the long road. It is a shield, permissible for a short time only. In the end one has to discard shields and remain open and vulnerable. Otherwise, scar tissue will seal off the wound and no growth will follow. To grow, to be reborn, one must remain vulnerable – open to love but also hideously open to the possibility of more suffering.[10]

Grieving cannot be a quick, brave, tearless thing. It takes time and space. To come to grips with feelings of loss, vacancy, or emptiness is essential. We need time to grasp an irreversible change that has taken place.

Grieving is a very personal process. Some people seem to work through their grief in a matter of weeks; others may take months or years. In my experience, even for those who seem to have recovered outwardly within a short period of time, the grief usually continues in subtle ways for a long time.

Sometimes a grieving person just cannot bring himself to accept the finality of loss. Sometimes, too, he may be tempted to rebel at the burden of suffering, to blame God for taking away a loved one, and to sink into deep despair. Then intense but patient spiritual support is needed.

Many people find that visiting the grave of a loved one brings comfort. We remember the smiles and laughter, the struggles and joys, and we look forward to the time when we will be together again.

Recently a woman wrote to me after her sister died:

> It is not easy to go on after you have lost someone very close, to get back into the everyday things of life after you have experienced eternity coming down right into your family. On the one hand you have to keep going and continue to affirm life. On the other, you have to allow the pain of death to soften your heart. You also have to take time to let the experience speak to you and change your life. It must have a purpose, and it is a danger to harden yourself rather than let the pain deepen your faith.
>
> In a way, I feel that it can even be a gift to have a family member in heaven – it brings one much closer to the other world, and you feel almost as if yourself are living partly in heaven already.

In these last weeks we have gone again and again to that peaceful spot where she lies. I cannot describe the comfort we gain from sitting at the graveside of one so dearly loved.

There is a strange comfort in being close to a loved one even before burial: I will never forget, for instance, how much it meant to me to prepare my father's body for burial together with Milton Zimmerman, a fellow Bruderhof member and Papa's doctor. This last service of love for the departed should be part of every family's grieving process, yet it is hardly practiced anymore – in fact, it has become seen as a distasteful task for the mortician. I think family members are missing out on something of profound importance.

In general, age-old burial customs are disappearing, partly because of a dwindling faith in God. Since time immemorial, the burial place has been revered as sacred ground. Yet even in places like Germany, a country whose customs are steeped in religious tradition, there is a trend away from regarding the grave as a precious site. Quite apart from repeated instances of willful desecration, growing numbers of people there choose to be buried anonymously, without even a parting farewell from relatives. One wonders why. Did they regard themselves as burdensome; did they feel that they were only tolerated and not loved? That there was no hope of being remembered after their death? Somehow, it seems to me that an anonymous grave is a testimony to little more than wretchedness and despair, and to the failure of the living to have shown adequate love.

IN EVERY PERSON there is a God-given, innate longing to know that he belongs to someone, that he is cherished and will be remembered. Just as every child needs the security of family, every elderly person pines for love and for a sense of belonging. Let us never fail to draw them close to our hearts while they are still alive, so that they may die and be buried with the love and dignity they deserve as beings created in God's image.

After a funeral the emptiness of the bereaved may be almost unbearable. Let the tears come; they are not a sign of weakness, but of being human. God is there for you. Revelation tells us that "he will dry your tears and heal all your sorrows" (Rev. 21:4). To some, a surprising strength is given in the first days after death that helps them cope with their loss, but even to these, the full impact will come sooner or later. In fact, the pain may even intensify as time goes on. Thus, the grieving must be able to talk about their feelings of sadness, anger, numbness, and other emotions that overwhelm them.

It is tragic when people feel too embarrassed or inhibited to share their grief. Why can't we let down our guard and admit that it takes a long time to accept our loss? Often it is helpful for the family and others who were close to the deceased to share their memories – to laugh and cry together. Writing down these memories can be a comfort for hard times ahead. Simply sitting together in silence can also be a great help. A woman once told me that after her father died, she went to my parents, sobbing, and poured out her need. They simply listened, and then my father said, "I understand." That was all. But it meant more to her than all the words of wisdom and advice others had given.

The necessity of sorting through the clothing and belongings of a recently departed one is always painful, but it can also be an occasion for healing. When Delf and Katie (a Canadian couple who joined the Bruderhof) lost their two-year-old son Nicholas in a car accident, they went through their neighborhood from house to house, sharing their pain and grief. As hearts were touched and lives were changed the tragedy became a positive experience; agnostics became believers, and those who believed were led to deeper faith. Some time later the parents brought Nicholas's clothes and toys to a poor couple in their neighborhood who had a child the same age. Healing can come through acts of love.

After a death, and especially after a long period of extended care, those who have been closest to the deceased will find that the whole focus of their life seems to be gone. Sometimes they will need to be helped to find a new focus, a practical outlet for their creative energies. When the German composer Johannes Brahms wrote his *Requiem* in the

1860s, he was mourning the death of his mother. Less concerned with setting to music the usual prayers for the dead than with finding comfort, he selected verses from Scripture that speak of hope: "Blessed are they that mourn," "Sorrowing and sighing shall flee away forever," "How lovely is thy dwelling place, O Lord of hosts," "The souls of the righteous are in the hand of God." Brahms's productivity at this time of his life surely helped him find healing and gave him a creative outlet for his grief.

Some people I have known find that accompanying another person through grief has a healing effect on their own lives. In an earlier chapter I told about Merrill. Several months after his death, his widow Kathy traveled to one of our communities to support another woman who had lost her husband. Kathy told me later that instead of reviving her pain, this experience was a blessing that brought closure to her own grief.

No MATTER how well one is able to come to terms with the loss of a loved one, there will always be moments when the heart feels tugged – perhaps by an anniversary, perhaps by a seemingly unrelated event that triggers an old memory. At times like these it is important to pause and allow oneself time for reflection.

I never knew my grandfather, but I knew my grandmother and (of course) my parents. On the anniversaries of their deaths each year, I am reminded of how much their lives meant and still mean to me personally, and to many others, and I think of the wonderful words in Revelation, "Blessed are they who die in the Lord, for their works follow after them." These words are inscribed on the gravestones of my father and grandfather.

At burial services in our communities, we are reminded that when we give the bodily remains over to the earth, we are not saying good-bye for ever; we do it in the certainty of resurrection. Though there is pain at the present, God's future holds out a promise – however unexplainable and mysterious – to which we can cling. As Jane Clement writes:

> We shall be circled over at length
>   by a remoter sky,
> And flung into a starrier space
>   more deep, more high.
>
> Some day the little mind of man
>   will crack and spin
> to let the chattering years fly out,
>   forever in.
>
> The sea will be more brief to us
>   than jewel of rain;
> and what now stuns us with its might,
>   beauty or pain,
>
> will be as faint as cheep of mouse
>   or swing of flower

under the gusty wing of heaven;
    and what seems power

will drop away and pale to dust
    held in the palm;
and what seems passion now will sink
    to leveled calm.

Therefore be quiet with your breath,
    all little men,
and hold some wonder in the Now
    for the Great Then.

22 Resurrection

"WHY DO YOU SPEAK about death as 'passing into eternity?'" a child once asked me. Our flesh, blood, and bones are not, in the truest and deepest sense, our real selves. The real seat of our being is our soul, which will not die but will truly pass from time into timelessness, from mortal life to immortality. God is the author of our souls, and our souls are constantly drawn back to him. Despite the busyness of our lives and our wayward natures, our souls yearn, deep down, for God and for eternity.

Throughout time and across all cultures men and women have been preoccupied with life after death and with varying ideas as to what form it may take. I would never presume to explain resurrection, but I am convinced of this: to believe in it, one must be conscious of the greatness of God. God's thoughts move in a completely different dimension than our thinking. We who live in time and

space have only an inkling of the meaning of eternity –
"For now we see through a glass darkly" – but if our hearts
are open, we can find ways of understanding it that tran-
scend any need to explain it intellectually. Miracles of
resurrection are all around us – in the transformation of
caterpillar into butterfly, of waterworm into dragonfly,
of seed into flower. And we have Paul's promising words:

> Lo! I tell you a mystery. We shall not all sleep, but we
> shall all be changed, in a moment, in the twinkling of
> an eye, at the last trumpet. For the trumpet will sound,
> and the dead will be raised imperishable, and we shall
> be changed (1 Cor. 15:51–52).

I remember vividly the first time I heard the story of the
crucifixion from my father. My heart rebelled – I could not
accept the fact that Jesus had to suffer as he did. I could
not believe that people could be so cruel. I wanted the
resurrection without the crucifixion. It was Easter, and on
Good Friday the bells never rang; everyone was serious and
solemn. Then, on Easter morning, we were awakened by
singing: "Christ the Lord is risen today!" What a difference
in the faces of the grown-ups! It took years, but little by
little, the truth began to make sense to me and echo in my
heart: just as spring must be preceded by winter; just as the
sunrise is glorious because it breaks through the dark of
night, so must death and suffering come before the tri-
umph of resurrection.

Hand in hand with our belief in resurrection goes our
certainty that, when the time is fulfilled, Christ will bring

in his kingdom. My parents told me more than once about Jabez, a ninety-two-year-old who joined our community in England around 1940. Jabez seems to have left an indelible impression on those who knew him. A white-bearded, patriarchal figure who loved to sit in his chair and look out over the ripening fields outside his room, he often spoke of God's great harvest to come. Here was a man who lived in daily expectation of the coming kingdom and who, like Simeon, was given in his old age a glimpse of eternal glory breaking in on earth.

Numerous passages in the Bible speak of man's longing for a Messiah, a Redeemer. This longing is fulfilled in Christ. He came to us – and comes to us again and again – with the promise of eternal life. His promise has one vital condition: as we live, so shall we die. Yet in the end, it is our *living,* not our dying, that counts. As the Indian mystic Sundar Singh says:

> It is easy to die for Christ. It is hard to live for him. Dying takes only an hour or two, but to live for Christ means to die daily. Only during the few years of this life are we given the privilege of serving each other and Christ…We shall have heaven forever, but only a short time for service here, and therefore we must not waste the opportunity.[11]

23 Fulfillment

THERE ARE TWO KINDS of death: physical and spiritual. The first is inevitable; the second is not. Everyone fears death, but God promises us that if we place our trust in him, he will give us strength to rise above our fears. His eternal love will be with us to our last hour.

The best preparation for dying is living a fulfilled life. If we live our lives faithfully, in service to others, we need not fear death. Those who have lived for selfish pursuits will always be haunted by death and dread its approach. Think of Charles Dickens's character Marley: "dead as a doornail," he dragged a chain that he himself had forged, link by link, with his miserly deeds. Scrooge forged a similar chain because he closed his heart to love and despised his fellow human beings. Then he changed. Realizing how selfish his life had been, he made a conscious choice: "It is time to make amends."

It is never too late to change. Consider the thief crucified with Christ: only hours before his death he repented, and Christ assured him that he would rest in Paradise. Think also of those whose stories I have recounted in this book. Perhaps the deepest message they leave each of us is the challenge to use our time on earth to live for love. They remind us, too, that indeed none of us knows the hour of his or her parting.

Every death brings a message for the living. Do we listen? How many of us consider the gravity of death? We prefer to push it aside, to forget about it and go on with our lives. Death is always a shaking experience, and we do not want to be shaken. Yet shouldn't its finality call to us to change our lives while there is still time?

When our physical lives end, our achievements will mean nothing unless they have been infused with love. As the Apostle Paul tells us, the greatest of all gifts is love. By love I do not mean a mere emotion. True love is a practical reality. It is work; it is deeds. Love leads to forgiveness, and forgiveness to peace. That is why God commands us to forgive others – so that we ourselves can be forgiven. Important as this is for all of our life, it is most important at the hour of our death. Those who are confident of having received forgiveness for their wrongs and of having forgiven those who have hurt them will be spared the final hours of anguish. They will be able to spend their last minutes in peaceful anticipation of the new life awaiting them.

I believe that when our last breath is drawn and our soul meets God, we will not be asked how much we have accomplished. We will be asked whether we have loved enough. That is why St. John of the Cross says, "In the evening of life, we shall be judged by love."

Someone once asked my great-aunt Else on her deathbed if she had any special wish. She replied simply, "Only to love more." If we live our lives in love, we will know the mystery of God's peace at the hour of death. And we will have no fear.

Afterword

IN HIS BOOK *The Denial of Death,* Ernest Becker
argues that all of us are afflicted with the dread of dying.
This common anxiety may be pushed aside by activities
and diversions of every conceivable kind. Yet however
successfully suppressed, it lurks in the soul, ready to leap
out at any moment.

One of my friends, a professor of psychiatry, insists that
an emotionally mature individual will suppress this dread
and realistically face the inevitable end of his life in this
world. However, since that ending may be preceded by
prolonged incapacitation and unrelievable agony, there is
still, even among the most courageous, a lingering fear, if
not of death itself, then still of the process by which we
make our passage down into the dark.

Perhaps this is why I was so moved by the stories in this
book, so much so that I immediately gave the unfinished

manuscript to a dear friend of mine, who from all indications is on the threshold of eternity.

Johann Christoph Arnold's words cannot but be a great blessing to those who suffer and battle against death's encroachment. While the pilgrims who related their experiences here are truthfully realistic, they bear a joyful testimony to the mystery of God's sustaining grace, his comforting presence, and the hope-giving strength of the Gospel. Indeed, they assure us that faith is the antidote for this common dread.

Here, then, is a book I have found (and will continue to find) to be invaluable in my counseling and pastoral ministry. It is a wonderful witness of how the fear of dying need not have the final word. It stirs, yes awakens, the soul, not only of those who nervously avoid the question of death – or of those who care for the terminally ill – but of us all.

Vernon Grounds
Denver Seminary

The Author

Johann Christoph Arnold has served as senior elder of the Bruderhof Communities (approximately 2,500 members) since 1983. He has traveled the world extensively on behalf of the movement and met with religious leaders of many faiths.

Over the years Christoph and his wife, Verena, have counseled hundreds of couples, single men and women, and teenagers, including inmates in several prisons; they have also provided pastoral care for the terminally ill and their families – many of whose stories are related in this book.

At first glance, Christoph might seem no different from any other author writing on death and dying – or marriage, parenting, or any other issues – from a biblical perspective. Yet his message is hardly typical. Perhaps that is because it is grounded in truths lived out for generations at the Bruderhof, a community movement based on Christ's teachings in the Sermon on the Mount and on the practices of the early believers in Jerusalem, as described in the Book of Acts. In a sense, Christoph's books are more than books; they bring to expression the life and faith of a whole church.

Christoph is editor-in-chief of *The Plough,* the Bruderhof's quarterly journal on spiritual and social transformation, and the author of seven other books: *A Plea for Purity, A Little Child Shall Lead Them, Seventy Times Seven, Seeking Peace, Cries from the Heart, The Lost Art of Forgiving, and Drained.* An active speaker, he has appeared as a guest on numerous television and radio programs, and on seminary and college campuses. Christoph welcomes responses to his books. Write to him at Plough using the address on the back cover.

Endnotes

1. Eberhard Arnold, *The Early Christians After the Death of the Apostles.* (Rifton, NY: Plough, 1970), 181.

2. Stephen B. Oates, *Let the Trumpet Sound: The Life of Martin Luther King, Jr.* (New York: Harper & Row, 1982), 486.

3. Karl Noetzel, ed., *Leo Tolstoi: Religiöse Briefe.* (Sannerz, Germany: Gemeinschafts-Verlag Eberhard Arnold, 1923), 20–21.

4. George Macdonald, *Weighed and Wanting.* (Boston: D. Lothrop & Company, 1882), 520.

5. Eberhard Arnold, *The Early Christians.* (Rifton, NY: Plough, 1970), 68–70.

6. Ibid, 176.

7. From a speech by Mother Teresa at the National Prayer Breakfast in Washington, D.C., February 1995.

8. *Journal of the Royal Society of Medicine,* February 1996.

9. Stanley Vishnewski, comp., *Meditations* [by Dorothy Day]. (New York: Newman Press, 1970), 43.

10. Anne Morrow Lindbergh, *Hour of Gold, Hour of Lead: Diaries and Letters of Anne Morrow Lindbergh, 1929–1932.* (New York: Harcourt Brace Jovanovich, 1973), 215.

11. T. Dayanandan Francis, ed., *The Christian Witness of Sadhu Sundar Singh, A Collection of his Writings.* (Madras: The Christian Literature Society, 1989), 577.